Research and Development for the NHS

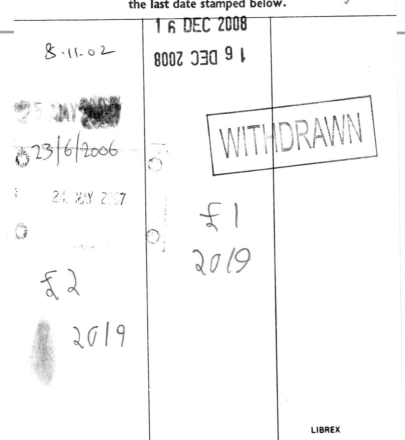
The COMET Library
Luton & Dunstable Hospital
NHS Trust, Lewsey Road
LUTON LU4 0DZ

Tel: 01582 497201
E-mail: library@ldh.nhs.uk

Radcliffe Medical Press Ltd
18 Marcham Road, Abingdon, Oxon OX14 1AA, UK

First edition 1996
Second edition 1998

British Library Cataloguing in Publication Data

A catalogue record for this book is available from the British Library.

ISBN 1 85775 402 6

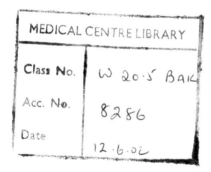
Typeset by Advance Typesetting Ltd, Oxon
Printed and bound by TJ International Ltd, Padstow, Cornwall

Contents

Foreword

The tasks facing those working in health and healthcare are exciting but challenging. The government's commitment to modernising the NHS through the NHS Plan offers great opportunities for change and improvement. We need to transform our approach to the quality of care that patients receive, through the implementation of clinical governance and other parts of the 'quality agenda'. And we must keep our eyes on the longer-term goals of improving public health and reducing health inequalities.

One way of achieving these goals is by making greater use of relevant, high-quality research-based evidence. That is why the NHS R&D programme is so vital and why recent changes to the programme – discussed in detail in this important book – have been so helpful. Three changes are of particular significance. First, the establishment of the Service Delivery and Organisation Programme, looking at a hitherto under-researched area of healthcare. Second, the linking of some of the outputs of the Health Technology Assessment Programme to the work of the National Institute for Clinical Excellence, helping to close the loop between research and practice. Third, the changes in the funding of NHS R&D, ensuring greater transparency and a greater sensitivity to the priorities and needs of the NHS. Taken together, these changes will help to ensure that the R&D programme promotes research that is rigorous, relevant and – most important – used by decision makers.

I therefore warmly welcome the publication of this third edition of *Research and Development for the NHS*. The editors and authors, who have wide experience in NHS management, NHS R&D and health services research, have produced a book that will be of value to anyone wanting to understand how the R&D programme currently works, how it is responding to the changing NHS, and how it is bringing the benefits of research to healthcare practice and delivery.

Professor Liam Donaldson
Chief Medical Officer
March 2001

List of contributors

Mark R Baker Medical Director, North Yorkshire Health Authority

Cliff Bailey Regional Director of Research and Development, NHS Executive Northern and Yorkshire

David Braunholtz Senior Research Fellow in Statistics, Department of Public Health and Epidemiology, University of Birmingham

Harry Cayton Chief Executive of the Alzheimer's Society. Member of the Central Committee on Research & Development in the NHS and Vice Chair of Consumers in NHS Research

Maureen Dalziel Director of the National Co-ordinating Centre for NHS Service Delivery and Organisation Research and Development

Brian Ferguson Professor of Health Economics and Head of Research, Nuffield Institute for Health, University of Leeds

Antony Franks Senior Lecturer in Public Health, University of Leeds and Medical Director, Laboratory Radiology and Pharmacy Services, Leeds Teaching Hospitals NHS Trust

John Gabbay Professor of Public Health, Wessex Institute for Health Research and Development

Hugh Gravelle Associate Director Research and Development, National Primary Care Research and Development Centre, Centre for Health Economics, University of York

Bec Hanley Director of the Consumers in NHS Research Support Unit

Stephen Harrison Professor of Social Policy, University of Manchester

Lynn Kerridge Programme Manager, National Co-ordinating Centre for Health Technology Assessment, Wessex Institute for Health Research and Development, University of Southampton

Jos Kleijnen Director, Centre for Reviews and Dissemination, University of York

Simon Kirk Assistant Director, Public Health and Clinical Governance, North Yorkshire Health Authority

Richard Lilford Regional Director of Research and Development, NHS Executive West Midlands Regional Office

Peter Littlejohns Clinical Director of the National Institute for Clinical Excellence

Ruairidh Milne Scientific Director, National Co-ordinating Centre for Health Technology Assessment, Wessex Institute for Health Research and Development, University of Southampton

Iain J Smith Senior Lecturer, Health Services Research, Nuffield Institute for Health, University of Leeds

Ken Stein Consultant in Public Health Medicine, North and East Devon Health Authority

David Wilkin Associate Director Research and Development, National Primary Care Research Centre, University of Manchester

I

The NHS R&D strategy

SIMON KIRK

The top doctors obtained *à la suite* terms in the Health Service: part-time payment for loosely defined sessions, the secret disposal of Treasury funds to those of their number whom Lord Moran and his two colleagues thought more meritorious, the lion's share of the endowments of the teaching hospitals to pay for their researches, and the right to private practice – much as before. The consultants had gained regular remuneration without any loss of freedom and were being trusted to use this freedom responsibly.[1]

From assumptions through vision to modernisation

In terms of research and development (R&D), the settlement negotiated between the State and the medical profession at the inception of the NHS persisted for 43 years. It took 40 of those years before the authoritative voice of the House of Lords set out what was really wrong with NHS R&D. After a brief 'visionary' period with Professor (later Sir) Michael Peckham at the helm – with cross-party support – the 1997 Labour government returned to the 1988 themes set out by their Lordships with its further 'modernisation' of R&D funding.

Assumptions

Health services operate on the basis of assumptions. These assumptions cover just about the entire range of the NHS, from its organisation and management to its clinical content and the delivery of the resulting healthcare to the population. Assumptions, by their very nature, are inexplicit. They are the 'common-sense' currency in which we trade.

One such is that the NHS, or more particularly the clinical professions within it, 'do' research and, to a lesser extent, the other half of the R&D equation – development. Like all common-sense notions, the assumption that the NHS has always included R&D is not entirely without foundation. The teaching hospitals and university-linked medical posts have always provided evidence of research output, whilst the other clinical professions have sought parity of esteem through similar intellectual endeavour. Meanwhile the Medical Research Council (MRC), alongside the other national research councils, has developed its empire of the basic biomedical sciences, ably assisted by the major medical research charities. Similarly, each of the Royal Colleges and most of the other bodies of professional representation has been more or less systematic in their individual pursuit of research and development goals. In addition, the Department of Health and its predecessors have a long-standing tradition of reactive research funding and of central research commissioning. However, the whole never quite seemed to be greater than the sum of its parts.

Towards vision

This non-directed approach to the doing of research has produced a series of problems recognised for decades. In 1988 the House of Lords Select Committee on Science and Technology published its report *Priorities in Medical Research*, which criticised the NHS for failing both to articulate its research needs and attend to the problems of implementation.[2] With the possible exception of the defence industries, British science in all its many guises has arguably suffered from the worst effects of *laissez-faire* attitudes. Consequently, and probably more importantly, the utilisation of scientific evidence, near-scientific evidence and the otherwise justifiable, has been considerably poorer than it ought to have been. In the NHS context this *laissez-faire* approach has been significant in enabling continuing variations in professional practice and service organisation, and thus the health both of the population and individual patients.

Forty-three years after its inception, the NHS appointed its first National Director of R&D, Professor Sir Michael Peckham. The basis of his manifesto for coherence was in part identified and trailed by the Department of Health in the preceding year's publication *Taking Research Seriously*.[3] This report, commissioned to consider how to improve the use and dissemination of research, stated 'Overall, there is a need for a clear *commitment* to research, with resources provided for its dissemination and responsibility taken for its use'. The recommendations of the report were addressed to three specific audiences and are identified in Boxes 1.1–1.3: those responsible for the central commissioning of research, those responsible for managing it and those undertaking it. Although focused on the dissemination of research findings, the recommendations continue to make salutary reading.

Box 1.1: Policy divisions *should*:

- commission research which is likely to be useful
- specify clearly the aims of individual studies
- clarify the products wanted from each study
- take an active interest in the research sponsored
- help to disseminate research findings
- consider the employment of specialist staff to advise on research
- commission focused reviews of existing research.

Box 1.2: Research management *should*:

- develop a strategic approach to research management and use
- include a dissemination period in research contracts and provide resources for dissemination
- advise customers on research that may be useful
- assess researchers on their dissemination efforts
- establish a dissemination database.

Box 1.3: Researchers *should*:

- take principal responsibility for dissemination
- write time for dissemination into research plans and proposals
- complete specified reports on time
- ensure that publications are clearly targeted to specific audiences
- prepare attractive and accessible material
- produce and distribute summaries of their research
- disseminate research imaginatively and widely.

Vision

The 'R&D challenge' was taken up on the appointment of Professor Peckham and the April 1991 announcement of an R&D strategy for the NHS. His proposals for a strategic approach were first publicly delivered in June 1991 at the Royal College of Physicians and published in *Lancet*.[4] He introduced his proposals thus:

A research approach has not been brought to bear systematically on issues relating to the effectiveness of clinical practice, the dispersal and use of existing knowledge, the best use of human and other resources, and the contributions of medical interventions to the health status of individuals and the population. Neither has there been a systematic attempt to relate important health issues to the national effort in medical research ... . The challenge now is to introduce a sensible mechanism for handling within the NHS the output of basic and applied research and to apply research methods to examine the content and delivery of health care. Such a mechanism is the only way of resisting the sometimes unreasonable and often unproven resource-consuming demands of lay, professional, and industrial pressure groups.

Specific objectives were clarified and mechanisms identified with the publication of the 1991 strategic statement *Research for Health*.[5] The three major objectives were: to make NHS decision making research based; to provide the NHS with the capacity to identify problems appropriate for research; and to improve the relationship of the NHS with the science base as a whole, rather than solely with medical research.[6]

The scope of the new NHS R&D programme was, and remains, deliberately broad, encompassing in various degrees every aspect from basic research to routine application (*see* Figure 1.1) and is consistent with the desire to improve overall co-ordination of health research (*see* Figure 1.2). Within the NHS, the strategy sought to improve the quality and

Figure 1.1 Basic research to routine application. (Adapted from *Research for Health* (1991) Department of Health, London, pp. 4–5.)

appropriateness of research, the effectiveness of development, the stability of the R&D infrastructure, the consistency of R&D education and training (including that which enables a proper appreciation of R&D) and to secure the resources necessary for these tasks.

Within two years the Director of R&D was able to report an exciting degree of progress that had, over and above the specific tasks outlined, begun to impact on the consciousness of the NHS.[7] Such impact would not have been possible without an improved degree of clarity. A particularly necessary

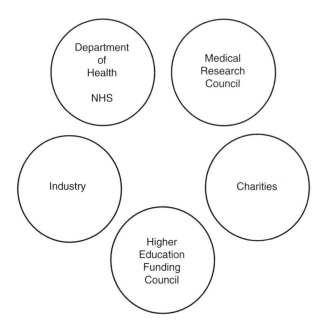

Figure 1.2 Co-ordination of health research. (Adapted from *Research for Health* (1991) Department of Health, London, p. 3.)

area of clarity has been achieved by defining what exactly constitutes NHS R&D (*see* Box 1.4).

The achievement and confirmation of such clarity was all the more remarkable given that it occurred during yet another of the cycles of change that constantly absorb the energy of the NHS in general and its management in particular. The publication of the Culyer Report[8] (discussed in more detail elsewhere) provided a detailed schema for the support of NHS R&D, comprising: a clear separation (and thus both accountability and guaranteed continuity in the internal market) for R&D funding; a clear requirement for those undertaking R&D to justify their continuing receipt of support; and a guarantee of equal access to R&D funds for the primary and community care sectors alongside that of the acute sector.

Box 1.4: Definition of NHS R&D developed under the NHS R&D strategy with the advice of the Central Research and Development Committee

'All research and development whose direct costs are met with NHS funds should:

- be designed to provide **new knowledge** needed to improve the performance of the NHS in improving the health of the nation

- be designed so that findings will be of value to those in the NHS facing similar problems outside the particular locality or context of the problem, i.e. be **generalisable**

- follow a clear, well defined **protocol**

- have had the protocol **peer reviewed**

- have obtained the approval, where needed, of the **Local Research Ethics Committee** and any other appropriate body

- have clearly defined arrangements for **project management**

- plan to report findings so that they are open to critical examination and accessible to all who could benefit from them – this will normally involve **publication**.'

(Reproduced from *Supporting research and development in the NHS (the Culyer Report)*, 1994.[8])

In addition, the regional leadership which developed under the auspices of the first two editions of *Research for Health* was confirmed despite the subsequent dissolution of the regional health authorities (RHAs) and the creation of NHS Executive (NHSE) regional offices (ROs). Abolition of RHAs reduced the excitement fashioned in the early years but consistency was assured. The new regional structures were described in a joint Department of Health and NHSE guide to R&D functions and responsibilities in the (then) 'new' NHS,[9] designed to accompany the 1994 R&D plans of RHAs and clarify responsibility for the co-ordination and management of work within the R&D strategy.

The Department of Health's Director of Research and Development is a member of the NHS Executive Board and is supported by an NHS Executive Branch of the Department's R&D Division. Within the NHS Executive, staff to support the R&D strategy are located in the headquarters and each regional office. Each of the regional offices have continued to include a Regional Director of R&D as part of the top management team, along with supporting staff, whose primary responsibilities relate to the R&D strategy and the continuing development of regional networks to ensure its success.

Modernisation

In retrospect it has to be acknowledged that the R&D strategy alone was never going to take the NHS to the brink of a major cultural transformation. Nevertheless, it did have a major influence on arguments for a more rational approach to that least rational of things – the provision of healthcare services through human interaction within a complex network of ever more complex organisations.

It does seem, however, to have been successful in shaping at least the aspiration to rationality within an even more complex system – that which governs the choices made by national politicians on behalf of the public. The following chapters describe the range of impacts that the R&D strategy has and continues to have. Most notable of all has been the apparent end of strategy and its continuation by technocracy. By this is meant the fact that there has not so far been a *Research for Health 3* published by the government (and at the time of writing none looks likely). Whilst endless sequels can undoubtedly become tediously repetitive, it is notable that the current government has chosen to publish instead a 'statement of policy and principles, and a development programme for NHS R&D Funding' under the title *Research and Development for a First Class Service: R&D funding for the new NHS*.[10] Ministerial priorities are summarised in the Foreword thus:

This country has an outstanding record of scientific innovation. In health, it rests on mutual support between the NHS, universities and bodies that fund high quality R&D. The reform of NHS R&D funding strengthens this partnership to keep our research at the forefront of relevance, quality and value. As well as providing solid support for the national science effort, the NHS must support R&D that is relevant to the national priorities of the NHS, responsive to the needs of those who use the NHS, its staff and decision makers, and accessible. It must take an integrated approach to securing the knowledge we need if we are to tackle health inequalities and provide effective modern health and social care.

To be fair, we are offered a restatement of Peckham's principles. This time, however, they have been wrapped in the language of technocratic reformism that characterises much of current governmental analyses. Whether the absence of passionate and highly visible political leadership is detrimental should be a consideration when reading the rest of this book.

References

1 Abel-Smith B (1964) *The Hospitals 1800–1948: a study in social administration in England and Wales*. Heinemann, London.
2 House of Lords Select Committee on Science and Technology (1988) *Priorities in Medical Research*. HMSO, London.
3 Department of Health (1990) *Taking Research Seriously*. HMSO, London.

4   Peckham M (1991) Research and development for the National Health Service. *Lancet.* **338**:367–71.

5   Peckham M (1991) *Research for Health.* Department of Health, London.

6   Smith R (1994) Filling the lacunae between research and practice: an interview with Michael Peckham. *BMJ.* **307**: 1403–7.

7   Peckham M (1993) *Research for Health.* Department of Health, London.

8   Culyer A (1994) *Supporting Research and Development in the NHS.* HMSO, London.

9   Department of Health and NHS Executive (1995) *Research and Development in the New NHS: functions and responsibilities*, Department of Health, London and NHS Executive, Leeds.

10 Department of Health (2000) *Research and Development for a First Class Service: R&D funding for the new NHS.* Department of Health, London.

2

R&D in the new NHS

MARK R BAKER

Introduction

During the turbulent years which followed the Conservative government's reform of the NHS, the NHS R&D strategy emerged as a unique unifying force. The strategy appeared to enjoy all-party political support, together with a desire for inclusion from all NHS organisations, the health professions and academic institutions. However, changes within the leadership of the strategy itself, successive changes in political leadership and a wholesale change in NHS policy has lead to a significant diminution in the influence of R&D in the NHS as a whole. In particular, the emerging desire of ministers to directly control all aspects of the NHS has forced the architects and leaders of the strategy to continually justify themselves, and has brought to a halt the increase in NHS funding in R&D that had persisted throughout most of the 1990s. Other chapters in this book describe in detail the profound changes in the way in which NHS R&D resources are to be utilised, together with changes in the relationship between NHS research funding and that of other research funders. In this chapter we will explore the strengths and weaknesses of the strategy during its first decade and how it has responded to the altered political environment.

Strengths and weaknesses

Overview

From the middle of the 1990s onwards, questions began to be asked about the return on investment in NHS R&D. To date, more than £4 billion of NHS funds have been spent on R&D and ministers and others are asking what impact this expenditure has had on the quality of NHS care. The charismatic and visionary leadership of the strategy provided by its first National Director, Professor Sir Michael Peckham, created a sense of purpose and direction during the early 1990s which was not sustained after his retirement. Peckham originally professed that to have a real impact on healthcare through an R&D strategy would take 20 years. To expect tangible returns after 5 years may seem unfair and optimistic, but early returns are an essential component of any tax-funded service and NHS R&D is no exception. The establishment and maintenance of national and regional structures has enabled the R&D strategy to withstand changes in political leadership and a very high turnover amongst national and regional directors. However, the extent of change in the NHS context and an increasing focus on delivering targets in operational services has relegated the essential long-termism of R&D to that of a support mechanism rather than a driver for change.

Of more importance for long-term success was the incorporation of a knowledge-based philosophy into the delivery of health services throughout the NHS. The appointment of R&D Directors in NHS Trusts and a major shift in investment into R&D in primary care has succeeded in stimulating the beginnings of a change of culture in the NHS. However, evidence of impact on NHS performance is hard to find and the increasing emphasis by government on achieving short-term targets to deliver political objectives is forcing advocates of R&D to continually justify the use of both resources and time on an enterprise which does not immediately deliver improvements in care.

Even within the framework of a knowledge-based NHS, the emphasis has shifted away from the acquisition of knowledge through primary research towards the dissemination and implementation of knowledge by dictat, for example through the outputs of the National Institute for Clinical Excellence (NICE) and National Service Frameworks. The process of clinical governance within all NHS provider organisations is a mechanism for ensuring that the outcomes of research are translated into practice in a consistent and universal manner, while the commitment to conducting primary research within the NHS itself has been altered. As described in Chapter 5, the use of NHS R&D funds to conduct own-account research, mainly by medical staff in hospitals, is being squeezed while a substantial investment is being made in co-ordinated cancer research, partly to increase the knowledge base for clinical cancer care but also significantly to harmonise practice by cancer clinicians.

Leadership and priorities

Drawing the medical profession into the heart of the R&D strategy at its outset was a prerequisite for the establishment of the status of the strategy. The vision of the strategy's architects involved the systematic implementation of the outcomes of research into practice and the behaviour of members of the medical profession was central to effecting those changes. An inclusive approach for medicine as a whole was therefore absolutely essential and almost all the Directors appointed in the early 1990s came from medical academic backgrounds. To a large extent this is still the case, although the present government has stimulated increasing professional democratisation with specific initiatives in R&D for other professions and a shift within medicine away from hospital specialties and towards general practice.

Setting of priorities for NHS R&D gave only token recognition to the interests of those who were not experts in the clinical field concerned. Managers and primary care professions were particularly marginalised and this seriously compromised the relevance of national R&D programmes to the issues facing services on the ground. A lack of dialogue between government, clinical constituencies and managers of the service has been a continuing concern, despite evidence from the USA that such an approach greatly strengthens the relevance and acceptance of research programmes. The obsession in the mid-1990s on establishing a funding system for R&D which matched the particular rules of the NHS market lead to the exclusion of health authorities themselves from most R&D decision making. This was even more perverse given that the R&D budget was effectively a levy on the funds available to health authorities.

Internationalism

It has been a matter of some pride for the Department of Health that no other nation has attempted what the NHS R&D strategy purports to do in England. To establish a comprehensive research strategy for a nation's healthcare system has made the NHS the envy of the developed world, in this regard at least. The investment in R&D infrastructure, especially the Centre for Reviews and Dissemination of the University of York and the UK Cochrane Centre at Oxford, gives the NHS R&D strategy both international prestige and a degree of leadership and acclaim. Early R&D investment has stimulated and supported international networks in research information and the establishment of NICE is a continuation of this theme. However, there remains a parochial tendency in health research in Britain, too often disregarding the results of international trials and replicating such work in an often inadequate way within the UK. These deficiencies apply to some reviews of research as well as to the conduct of clinical trials.

Little local difficulties

The enthusiasm with which the NHS R&D strategy was first met was accompanied by a number of parallel independent initiatives to join in the fun. For example, the development of the NHS Centre for Reviews and Dissemination and the UK Cochrane Centre to carry out secondary reviews of research and meta-analysis stimulated such work in many areas outside the quality control of those institutions. The quality of output was therefore as variable as the quality of the trials that were being reviewed. The *post hoc* establishment of standards for secondary reviews and the processes for commissioning reviews came later, and have now been reinforced by the co-ordination process under the auspices of NICE. These processes are described in more detail in Chapter 4. Early fragmentation of Health Technology Assessment (HTA) studies, including international duplication, has also been largely overcome by tighter co-ordination through the HTA co-ordinating centre (*see* Chapter 10). These deficiencies are not unique to the NHS R&D strategy but are common throughout the NHS, as they would tend to be in any organisation as large and fragmented as the NHS in England and Wales. The present government's reforms of the NHS, through *The New NHS* and *The NHS Plan*, have begun to address these systematic shortcomings through new structures and much tighter regulation, but these initiatives have yet to be proven.

The failure to communicate effectively both internally and externally has also been a deficiency of the R&D strategy. The stillborn National Project Register and failed communications within different divisions of the Department of Health all commissioning R&D in the same subject has led to both embarrassment and waste. The failure to deal systematically with the issues of dissemination and implementation for at least 7 years had proved a major frustration to all concerned with the strategy and with health services themselves. Most of these initiatives are now being addressed with significant hope of success. However, new challenges will arise in the future and the ability of the national leadership to respond promptly remains in doubt.

The early years of the strategy saw a consolidation of existing research expenditure and a minimal direction of funding to a small number of national programmes. The medical dominance of both the research and the setting of priorities has rendered much of this work valueless. In common with other government research funders, the bureaucracy associated with NHS R&D funding grants has irritated researchers and slowed up the whole process of generating knowledge promptly and efficiently. While successive governments have promised to reduce bureaucracy, increased external regulation invariably increases it.

The conundrum of evidence-based policy

Successive governments have adopted the slogan of evidence-based healthcare. The health professions have responded by demanding a similar approach to the policies that dictate the way they work. It is not usual in a democracy for parties to go into an election promising to conduct research into which policies they should adopt. Newly elected governments are therefore committed to implementing the changes on which they campaigned and they tend to show an unwillingness to invest in research to prove that their policies are wrong.

Nonetheless, changing the way in which the NHS delivers care is a knowledge-based issue. Research and development are required into better methods of delivering healthcare and of managing the resources tied up in healthcare. This research should properly be funded by the NHS itself; it is nobody else's business. The new National Programme on Service Delivery and Organisation (*see* Chapter 11) is now beginning to address some of these issues systematically. However, given the proximity of political control of NHS policy in management and the ever tightening political grip on short-term NHS performance, there remains a very high level of political sensitivity over any attempt to evaluate the consequences of this political control. Under our existing structures and political systems, it is difficult to envisage a solution to this conundrum.

Co-ordination

It is apparent to many observers that the NHS is simply too big to manage as a single organisation. The same is true of the knowledge-based infrastructure, which it is hoped will inform decision making at all levels of the NHS. It is hardly surprising therefore that it has proved frustratingly more difficult to pull together all the programmes, initiatives and themes of knowledge which have been generated directly by the NHS R&D strategy, all of which are relevant to implementing knowledge-based healthcare. The increasing use of electronic data transfer and virtual libraries are a means of making the evidence available to users of information with time and motivation to search, but there remains no central resource of assembled intelligence that can be easily accessed and analysed. The national electronic library for health may provide, in the course of time, the backbone for such a central resource but indexing and accessing will be a major undertaking. The portability of the Cochrane database makes a potentially invaluable tool in operational settings. These issues are discussed in more detail in Chapter 6.

Both the University Higher Education sector and the NHS have been unhealthily obsessed with competitiveness throughout most of the 1990s with the inevitable result that low value has been placed on co-operation and collaboration, despite the overwhelming evidence that partnerships flourish in both research and healthcare. Instead, excessive competition for resources has proved destructive and has served to distort priorities. The R&D strategy itself has not been the cause of these problems; indeed it is itself a victim of the prevailing culture of competitiveness between research groups, including health organisations. More recently, and especially since the publication of *The NHS Plan*, a significant move towards research networks involving all NHS organisations equally heralds a major change in the way in which research funds and research participation are applied. In common with other NHS strategies, it is now envisaged that all NHS organisations will participate in research and that all will do so to a high and comparable standard. NHS leaders are concerned over the historical competitiveness, and the tensions that it generated, while the R&D strategy is tolerated by clinicians and acknowledged as inevitable by managers but it is owned wholly only by the researchers. The NHS itself, which is supposedly the customer for the outputs of R&D, appears to have no more than observer status while also bearing the responsibility for meeting the costs of NHS R&D.

Management and leadership

The NHS R&D strategy now has its third National Director in Sir John Pattison. At each stage of its development, the strategy has had to be repositioned in the context of a new national director or a new Secretary of State for Health. Given that each of these changes is as imposing as a change of government, destabilisation is omnipresent in NHS R&D at the highest levels. Reorganisation and politics conspire to slow the pace of progress and even to reverse some elements of the R&D strategy. In the earliest days, Michael Peckham focused the management of the R&D strategy at the level of the regional health authority, those authorities being the only stable part of NHS management at the time. The continuing regional office role in R&D management, in succession to regional health authorities, recognises the relative stability of this tier but also removes it from the direct operation of the NHS. Indeed, the reorganisation of regional health authorities in 1994 and their absorption into the NHS Executive in 1996, while making sound sense for other reasons, proved destabilising and dysfunctional for research and development. New management, lost networks and reduced staff numbers led to lack of supervision of research and reviews in progress, waste and duplication, loss of quality and loss of focus. The removal of R&D management from the heart of the NHS operation has effectively severed the links with health authorities and with the mechanisms for determining local priorities.

To address these shortcomings, to extricate the R&D strategy from the fragmenting and dissolving NHS market and to recognise the major changes in NHS policy and political priorities following the election of a new government in 1997, the fundamental review of NHS R&D priorities, systems and frameworks was undertaken in 1998. The outcomes of this review for funding are described in detail in Chapter 5. Other aspects of this review have not yet been published in full by the government and may never be.

Implementing evidence-based healthcare

The responsibilities for generating knowledge and for implementing evidence-based healthcare have been split within the Department of Health. A lack of co-ordination between the two, together with the slowness of the professions to take up the mantle of evidence-based medicine in particular, have compromised the effective dissemination and implementation of the outputs of research. The exclusion of NHS management from the R&D strategy and the customary reluctance of the medical profession to change anything it does, have significantly contributed to a sense that the relationship between research and healthcare is optional. The present government have regarded this situation as completely unacceptable and have put in place a system of guidance, implementation and regulation which it expects to ensure will deliver consistent evidence-based healthcare throughout the NHS. This framework is described in more detail in the next chapter.

NHS management and R&D

NHS managers in general and health authorities in particular have remained marginal to the development of the R&D strategy. Token chief executives and senior directors have been included in regional and national committees, but there is no commissioning constituency in the strategy's frameworks and there is no real management ownership of the R&D strategy. Management organisations, such as the Institute of Health Service Management (IHSM) and the NHS Confederation, are not closely connected to the agenda and neither offers support or leadership to the NHS in this field or shows the inclination to regard the strategy as important. To some extent the lack of political leadership for R&D contributes to the low priority given to it by the Confederation. The NHS management community does not have any R&D standing groups and the strategy has managed to avoid most of the real managerial issues of the moment.

One of the basic problems is that managers do not know what they need to know and can often contribute relatively little to the real decision making. Indeed, the more the government dictates centrally to the NHS, the less likely it is that the NHS will attract managers able and willing to be as decisive as top managers need to be. Some top managers think that the R&D strategy will deliver a holy grail in the form of the 'big book of evidence-based commissioning' but this is an illusion. Management at the highest levels needs to move its ambitions from delivering the pointless but measurable, such as most government targets, towards the culture change that is necessary for a paradigm shift in rising standards, particularly amongst the clinical decision makers and leading to a health service that is rooted in evidence, responsiveness and with a passion for excellence.

Management of the NHS is not easy. Resource constraints, rising patient expectations and continuous political interference make the task of managing the nation's health service decreasingly rewarding and increasingly frustrating. A sound knowledge base is urgently required to support managers in effecting the changes that are required.

The Clarke review

Background to the review

The driving force for the review of NHS R&D by Michael Clarke was the abolition of the NHS internal market. The Culyer funding system, which had been in operation since

1996, was originally introduced to protect R&D funding from the effects of the internal market and to protect NHS providers from the costs of research impacting on their competitiveness within the market. With the abolition of the market all these issues were obsolete and therefore it was appropriate to reconsider the funding arrangements for NHS R&D. The processes and outcomes of the funding review are described in Chapter 5. At the same time, Clarke undertook a review of priority setting and the organisation of the research community within NHS R&D. It was recognised that, to secure closer political ownership of the R&D strategy, it was necessary to align R&D priorities more closely with political priorities.

Topic working groups

Multi-disciplinary groups were established to look at priorities for research in six key areas which resonated with wider government priorities for health and social care (*see* Box 2.1). These priorities do not cover the full list of national priorities for the NHS but they reflect the existence of National Service

---

Box 2.1: NHS needs and priorities for R&D topic working groups

- Cancer

- Cardiovascular disease and stroke

- Mental health

- Ageing

- Primary care

- Accidents.

Frameworks, or forthcoming frameworks, and other priorities for change in the NHS and further afield. The topic working groups themselves were broadly based but not always fully representative of the field. The initial tranche of priorities emerging from their deliberations therefore have significant gaps (for example no mention of radiotherapy in the cancer topic working group), and no such priority lists have been published so far. Periodic reviews of both the key topics and the priorities within each topic will be conducted from time to time.

In the first instance, funding priority will be given to cancer, cardiovascular disease and mental health and each of these now has a national R&D portfolio Director to co-ordinate NHS R&D activity in these areas. The commissioning of research in these priorities will be handled mainly by the Health Technology Assessment Programme and the Service Delivery and Organisation Programme (*see* Chapters 10 and 11).

An inclusive approach

Another outcome of the Clarke review is the incorporation of health authorities into the NHS R&D funding system for the first time. To reflect this, the R&D funding system now covers public health R&D and epidemiology as well as primary care research as part of the core NHS R&D strategy. A public health R&D strategy is to be published shortly. A consultation paper has recently been published on the introduction of the new arrangements for NHS priorities and needs R&D funding and it is anticipated that the new system will be operational from April 2001. Further priority topics will be subject to R&D leadership and advisory structures during 2001 and an annual cycle of reporting will be established thereafter.

Repositioning research and development

When the first edition of this book was written, research and development was seen as a major driver for change within the NHS. During the last 5 years, however, political factors have increasingly dominated and although knowledge continues to be a significant factor in determining progress of healthcare, its outputs are being continually co-ordinated by intermediate bodies such as NICE (*see* Chapter 4). It is therefore seen that organisations such as NICE and National Service Frameworks are the drivers for change with the research and development strategy supporting those systems rather than driving change itself.

The implementation of National Service Frameworks in particular has lead to the establishment of service networks, for example in cancer, and these networks are now being considered as a basis for R&D involvement as well. A cancer research network is being established throughout the NHS in England over a 3-year period, with a national co-ordinating centre and the inclusion of all 34 cancer networks into the organisation by 2003. £5 million is being top sliced from R&D funding to ensure the early success of this initiative with the objective of increasing the entry of patients into clinical trials by a factor of at least two. In addition to the increase in cancer clinical trial activity, it is well recognised that patients entered into trials, even in the control group, generally have better outcomes because of adherence to the protocols for care. The acquisition of knowledge through bigger, faster trials will of course be an asset to the NHS – and indeed to other health systems. An additional advantage of increasing the size of the cancer research framework within the UK would be to strengthen those health industries that fall outside the NHS. Of the greatest importance to the UK economy is the pharmaceutical industry, which has long campaigned for an increased use of chemotherapy within cancer care in the UK.

Substantial increases in the capacity of the NHS to participate in clinical trials in cancer is likely to attract pharmaceutical organisations to invest in this country and will encourage the early use of new cancer drugs in care in the NHS, the opposite of current practice and experience.

The Clarke review and its gradual implementation, together with a forthcoming election, should lead to a brief period of respite in the frenetic pace of change in NHS R&D. Establishment of the new systems, national programmes and R&D priorities will see the strategy through the next 3 years but is likely to undergo a further major review during the next parliament. The strategy currently enjoys good national leadership with effective co-ordination of national programmes and increasing resonance with government priorities. Compared with its heyday of the early 1990s, the strategy seems rather downbeat but its better connections, tighter management and more rational systems of funding will improve the return on investment, make it easier to demonstrate relevance to the NHS and political priorities and stands a better chance of surviving in the long term. But then, in politics, a week is a long time.

Further reading

- Department of Health (1997) *The New NHS: modern, dependable*. HMSO, London.
- Department of Health (2000) *The NHS Plan*. HMSO, London.

3

The new national agencies and R&D

MARK R BAKER

Introduction

The primary purpose of the government's White Paper *The New NHS* was to help extricate the NHS from its internal market and especially from GP fundholding. This was a primarily political objective and established new NHS structures such as Primary Care Groups in order to enable the new NHS to function. However, advantage was taken of the opportunity created by NHS reform to address a number of concerns raised during the previous decade by the professions, public and politicians. This chapter deals with the agencies, systems and processes that were established in 1998 to deal with these concerns.

Motivation for change

Variations in practice that were not justified by clinical needs have bedevilled healthcare in the NHS since its earliest days. *The New NHS* was illustrated with examples of such unjustified variations including survival from cancer, prescribing practices and surgical efficiency. The strategy of the day relied on releasing resources from improving the efficiency of those organisations below the top quartile in order to fund the improvements in services that were enjoyed by the best. The government described some of these variations as post-code prescribing and blamed the NHS market for their existence. In fact, such variations have always existed in the NHS and were due mainly to the personal preferences of doctors. To overcome these various problems, the government has established a range of new initiatives and agencies with the aspiration of all the services achieving the same high standards over a period of time and to eliminate variations in practice and performance that were not justified other than by exceptional circumstances.

A framework for quality

In the summer of 1998 the government published a con-sultation paper entitled *A First Class Service* which described in more detail than in the White Paper the role, structure and function of a number of new organisations and processes to achieve the goal of high and even quality of care. The frame-work is undoubtedly elegant and covers the full range of NHS activity from planning major service change to the treatment of individual patients. In terms of the organisation and delivery of services, the government will set out national standards for key areas of service in the form of National Service Frameworks. Local mechanisms are established for the implementation of these frameworks and service changes are described in the annual Health Improvement Programmes co-ordinated by health authorities. For clinical services and the management of individual patients, the National Institute for Clinical Excellence (NICE) will issue appraisals of health technologies and guidelines for the management of clinical conditions. Their implementation will be managed through the process of clinical governance. The competence with which the planning mechanisms for service change and the clinical mechanisms for improving clinical care are implemented will be assessed by the Commission for Health Improvement (CHI), a new regulatory agency which will conduct formal visits to every NHS organisation every 4 years and also act as a troubleshooting organisation to investigate specific incidents where practice falls significantly short of the standards expected.

The role of NICE is described in detail in the next chapter. As an agency designed to provide coherence and consistency from the evidence of efficacy and cost effectiveness, it is welcomed by all concerned. However, it is clear that the Institute is also being used by some as the often recommended fourth hurdle for pharmaceutical companies who must now not only demonstrate efficacy and safety but also the relative cost effectiveness of their therapies. At the time of writing, the Institute's rigour in this regard has yet to be tested as has the government's nerve in supporting negative recommendations from NICE about the use of expensive drugs with marginal benefits.

A National Service Framework (NSF) is the term used by the government to describe a set of standards, systems and processes to harmonise the quality and content of health services in complex areas. The prototype for this approach is the Calman–Hine Report on the commissioning of cancer services which was published in 1995. At the time, it was a backdoor attempt by the then Chief Medical Officers of England and Wales to try to improve health services for cancer despite the NHS market. The government of the day was persuaded against its better judgement to publish the report in fear of the publicity and professional backlash if it failed to do so. The process adopted for the Calman–Hine report and the detail of its conclusions are a pale shadow of the systematic and bureaucratic processes and the long and tortuous reports published since they acquired their new name and the nation a new government. Frameworks have been published for mental health and coronary heart disease and further frameworks for the care of older people and diabetes are currently being drafted. The arrangements for monitoring implementation are massively bureaucratic and appear to care little about the services that are supposed to be improved as a result. Vast quantities of public money are siphoned off the mainstream NHS budget in order to fund NSF implementation specifically. To date, they have done so in an unbalanced way and have significantly distorted funding allocations and local priorities. However, these are practical problems in what is essentially a sound strategy. Services should improve and they should be of equivalent content and quality. It is preferable if the changes proposed are backed by evidence and in some cases this is so. More often, however, the proposed changes are based on pragmatism or, worse still, political detail. It is envisaged that by 2005 there will be at least ten NSFs, some of them reviewed within that period. Money will be spent; services may improve; but the likeliest outcome will be the exhaustion of all concerned with their implementation.

The process known as clinical governance is essentially a framework for assuring the quality of clinical care. It is one of the most written about and spoken about changes in the NHS during the last 3 years and these writings and speeches are devoid only of understanding. While the goals of clinical governance are laudable and the principles sound reasonable, there is no evidence to suggest that a comprehensive system of governance will make a significant difference to outcomes. Government guidance on implementing clinical governance has been published and provides a response to the most common causes of service failure. These are evidence based in that the characteristics of failing organisations have been documented and potential causal elements have been identified. The strategies to improve these organisations are plausible but largely untested. Other initiatives, such as the formation of a national register of untoward events, and systems for supporting and assessing doctors who do not come up to scratch, constitute noble efforts to identify dangerous procedures and dangerous people, but they are reliant on the honesty and openness of the most closed profession in the world. Clinical governance is a good idea but whether it significantly contributes to improving the quality of care remains to be seen.

Health Improvement Programmes (HImPs) were introduced in the 1997 White Paper *The New NHS*, as the vehicle for providing a co-ordinated multi-agency and multi-sector response to the government's planning priorities. They were generally welcomed as a good idea and a necessary step to pulling together the disparate NHS organisations and local government partners in working together to improve health and social care. However, the continuous reorganisation of the NHS, especially the primary care sector, and the overwhelmingly centralised determination of priorities, processes and actions to meet equally centralised targets has seriously compromised the opportunity to use HImPs to improve local services as opposed to meeting remotely set priorities and targets. This is not to say that the work that has gone into developing HImPs has not been valuable in strengthening local partnerships and in achieving much greater ownership of the pressures and opportunities which confront public services. The problem is that obsessive centralisation has appeared to betray the investment of time and sovereignty made by local organisations in working together. While the first HImPs, published in 1999 were full of innovation and flexibility, subsequent Programmes are monitored only on the basis of whether they fully implement NSFs and other national priorities. Even partnerships themselves are now performance managed and the government's control freakery has even lead to their assumption that networks of care are themselves managed organisations. It is unlikely that the current administration can change its spots sufficiently to make HImPs the dynamic drivers for change in health services which their 1997 White Paper promised.

The CHI is the newest of the new agencies, established officially in April 2000. Although its functions and structure are described in some detail in *A First Class Service*, what it does and why, depend on who you are speaking to. The current batch of ministers look on the Commission as their troubleshooters, marching in to difficult situations and advising the minister on who should be sacked. From the Commission's leadership itself, one is likely to get an opinion that the Commission exists to raise the quality of healthcare by supporting health organisations to improve their overall managerial and clinical performance and to identify particular areas where improvement is needed. From the operational NHS's standpoint, an unsolicited visit from the Commission is to be avoided at all costs and a scheduled visit is a painful process to endure every 4 years. Evidence from other industries, including in the UK, suggests that external regulation doesn't work. The Commission would do far more for the NHS by concentrating on ensuring that local mechanisms, operating inside NHS organisations, were sufficiently robust to deliver the improvements in care that all stakeholders seek. It is the poisonous proximity of politicians to management of the NHS that will compromise its role and lead to the Commission becoming an object of fear, rather than support.

Health Development Agency

A similar approach has subsequently been adopted for public health and health promotion following the abolition of the Health Education Authority and its replacement by the Health Development Agency in 2000. Heralded in yet another White

Paper *Saving Lives: our healthier nation*, the Health Development Agency was formed from the remnants of the former Health Education body and is establishing a regional structure to support and inform its work.

Like its health service sisters, the Agency is designed to set standards for public health practice, to advise on developing public health workforce and to monitor progress in public health with the aid of the eight regional Public Health Observatories. It is in many ways a combination of NICE, CHI, NSFs and HImPs for the public health professions.

Perspectives on the quality initiative

There is no denying the elegance of the government's quality framework for the NHS. It is comprehensive, balanced, necessary and – in parts at least – adequately resourced. Its flaws lie not in its basic principles or structures but in the mode of its implementation and management.

All the elements of the framework described are separately managed. There is no overall leadership or umbrella management and the often pernicious influence of ministers is given too free a rein. It is a general rule that politicians make bad managers and managers make bad politicians. Political management of a system as complex as the NHS is bound to fail, regardless of the persistent tinkering with the structure, periodic confrontation with the professions and the attempts to empower the public. With all its advantages, a healthcare system in which users of service do not have a direct interest, for example through payment, is never going to fulfil all expectations. Political bullying without thanks or reward, whatever the sanctions, will not result in modernisation or excellence.

The individual elements of the quality framework have made a decent start. NICE has established sound systems and processes for technology appraisals and has, more or less, stuck to both its principles and its timetable. Technology guidance has been clear and easy to interpret though it remains to be seen if the same will be true of its guidelines. Clinical audit leadership is not yet apparent. Publicly apparent political interference has been minimal but there have been suggestions that an initially sceptical approach to the evidence concerning the use of taxanes in ovarian cancer was overturned after undisclosed pressure.

The CHI got off to an unsteady start, the Secretary of State sending them into a troubled Trust before the Commission legally existed. Political interference is likely to continue so long as ministers believe that a naming and shaming approach will benefit them electorally, always a doubtful strategy. Given the freedom it needs to support, instruct, develop and improve services, the Commission could become a major player in the NHS in the long term. The Director of its sister organisation OFSTED is probably the most powerful individual in the education sector. It is not impossible that the Director of Health Improvement, the title given to the managerial head of the Commission, will become equally powerful in the NHS.

NSFs have also had a rather mixed reception. The first NSF published with that title, in 1999, covered adult mental health. It was reasonably well received though rather unimaginative and not obviously evidence based. Arguments amongst the authors, and embarrassing political statements that harmed relationships with service users, damaged the process though probably not the outcome. Early evidence of implementation suggests an unhealthy obsession with process and a tendency to distort local priorities. The second NSF, on coronary heart disease, had an absurdly elongated gestation, the report sitting on ministers' desks for months prior to publication. The report changed little, providing ministers with an opportunity to spend a lot of money on revascularisation and promising the public a lot of benefits which the NHS is ill-equipped to deliver. Heated debate has occurred in the medical press about the obsolescence of the evidence used and not all clinicians agree with the balance of priorities. In general, however, the NSF is a good thing and will lead to raised standards of care, evidence-based practice and better outcomes. It will do little for research.

Clinical governance has so far achieved little other than to spawn an industry of conferences and books on how to do it by people who have, with few exceptions, never done it. The irritating probability is that the process of clinical governance, intended to avoid the service failures and personal deficiencies that have irritated ministers and angered the public, will have the opposite effect. It is already clear that the process will identify and expose systematic and individual failures and will further dent public and political confidence. How long, I wonder, will Ministers – and the Chief Medical Officer – be able and willing to dismiss the frequency of reported failures as part of a catching up process?

HImPs have great potential to bring together the full range of initiatives and developments in public services, which together, conspire to improve the health of the population. In many places, the new process has been used to strengthen local partnerships, whether or not the government has added the badge and the bribe of a Health Action Zone. The approach is pragmatic rather than empirical and the research into the effectiveness of the process is entirely qualitative. With the emergence and maturity of primary care groups, and the increasingly frenetic government initiative disease taking root, HImPs are poised to become little better than lists of government targets and local pretence at achieving them. Evidence, research, information and knowledge are extraneous luxuries.

The Health Development Agency is the youngest of the new bodies and has had little opportunity to have an impact yet. However, invisibility followed by episodes of excess has been characteristic of all its predecessors and there is no immediate reason to think that things will change much.

Conclusion

It is safe to assume that the quality framework and the new organisations will endure for some time. It is possible that a future Conservative government may be less enthusiastic about NSFs, which each commit a further billion pounds or so of public funds. We may assume that NICE and CHI will have a long-term future and that clinical governance and health improvement will exist at local level in some form or another. There is an urgent need for research into how to use these systems to add value but little likelihood of this field becoming a priority for R&D funding. There is also merit in acquiring national oversight and leadership of the whole quality initiative, bringing together the separate interests of the Chief Medical Officer, the Chief Nursing Officer and the Director of R&D.

Further reading

- Department of Health (1997) *The New NHS: modern, dependable*. HMSO, London.
- Department of Health (1998) *A First Class Service*. HMSO, London.
- Department of Health (1999) *Saving Lives: our healthier nation*. HMSO, London.

4

The relationship between NICE and the national R&D programme

PETER LITTLEJOHNS

The National Institute for Clinical Excellence (NICE) currently has no responsibility itself for undertaking research. Nevertheless the Institute is heavily dependent on the work of the research community and organisations responsible for the promotion of research especially the Research and Development Directorate of the National Health Service, the Medical Research Council, the Association of Medical Research Charities and the healthcare industries in order to fulfil its responsibilities. This chapter describes the work of the institute and the relationship it is developing with the R&D world in general and the NHS R&D programme in particular.

What is NICE?

The government's approach to improving the quality of the National Health Service (NHS) was initially made explicit in the white paper *The New NHS: modern, dependable*[1] with further details provided in *A First Class Service: quality in the new NHS*.[2] Standards were to be set at a national level through the creation of National Service Frameworks and the establishment of NICE.[3] At its most basic level the aim was to reduce the likelihood of unacceptable variation in the provision of care epitomised by the availability of expensive drugs in some health authorities and not in others. Putting an end to the 'the post-code lottery of care' was according to political pronouncements the *raison d'être* for the establishment of NICE.

However, there was a recognition that implementation of the emerging guidance would only be achieved if responsibility was taken at local level. Renewed emphasis was placed on establishing effective professional self-regulation and continuing professional development. Managerial commitment to quality improvement was sought through the development of clinical governance. Monitoring of the effectiveness of these approaches was to be undertaken through a number of mechanisms, which included creating the Commission for Health Improvement (CHI), working within a National Performance Framework (*see* Figure 4.1). While the approach was initially presented as a 'Quality Improvement' model with education and support being the key driving forces, over the last year mixed messages have been expressed by politicians. Breakdown of public and professional confidence in some of the current systems in place to assure professional standards has resulted in tougher messages from the government. However the institutions involved, CHI, NICE and the National Clinical Governance Support Team have gone out of their way to emphasise that their role is to support the NHS in addressing the daily challenges of delivering healthcare. This is particularly important when expectations and demand frequently exceed what is likely to be feasible within current service configurations.

NICE is a special health authority established on 1 April 1999. Its role is to provide national guidance on the clinical and cost effectiveness of clinical interventions. It achieves this through appraising new and existing technologies, developing clinical guidelines and supporting clinical audit. Details of all its activities are available on its website (www.nice.org.uk). Its specific advice will be incorporated into the broader organisational standards set by the National Service Frameworks. It is a small organisation (28 employees) and undertakes its work by commissioning and liaising with a range of professional, specialist and patient organisations. It is supported by its Partner's Council (which includes representatives from all its stakeholders including the Industry), a series of advisory committees and has formal links with a number of universities and the National Research and Development Programme. It works closely with local trusts and clinical governance professionals to ensure support for those responsible for implementing its guidance. This includes providing audit advice to accompany its guidance.

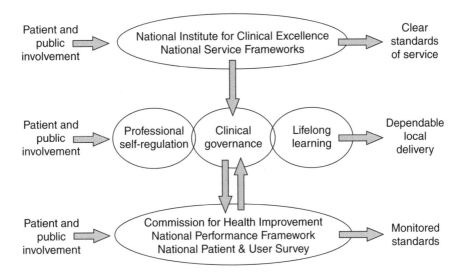

Figure 4.1 Setting, delivering and monitoring standards.

The NICE approach

The details of NICE's main work programmes for 1999–2000 and 2000–01 have been published.

Appraising health technologies:

The Department of Health and the National Assembly for Wales select technologies for appraisal by NICE based on a number of criteria.

- Is the technology likely to result in a significant health benefit, taken across the NHS as a whole, if given to all patients for whom it is indicated?

- Is the technology likely to result in a significant impact on other health-related government policies (e.g. reduction in health inequalities)?

- Is the technology likely to have a significant impact on NHS resources (financial or other) if given to all patients for whom it is indicated?

- Is NICE likely to be able to add value by issuing national guidance? For instance, in the absence of such guidance is there likely to be significant controversy over the interpretation or significance of the available evidence on clinical and cost effectiveness?

NICE follows a transparent and structured process for its appraisals (outlined in Figure 4.2), giving appropriate interested parties the opportunity to submit evidence, to comment on draft conclusions, and to appeal to a panel independent of those involved in the original judgement in

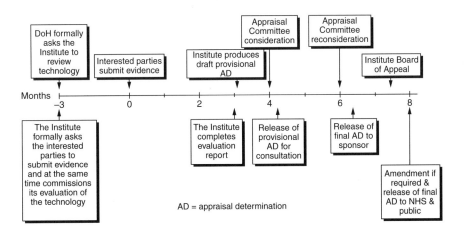

Figure 4.2 Diagrammatic representation of appraisal process.

cases where NICE is alleged to have: failed to act fairly; to have exceeded its powers; or to have acted perversely in the light of the evidence submitted. This is a dynamic process and is currently being reviewed after the experiences of the first year of appraisals.

NICE's function in relation to appraisals, as set out in the Secretary of State's directions, is 'to appraise the clinical benefits and the costs of such healthcare interventions and to make recommendations'. It assesses the evidence of all the clinical and other health-related benefits of an intervention, taking this in its widest sense, to include impact on quality of life, relief of pain or disability, etc., as well as any impact on likely length of life – to estimate the associated costs, and to reach a judgement on whether on balance this intervention can be recommended as a cost-effective use of NHS resources (in general or for specific indications, subgroups, etc.). Where there is already a cost-effective intervention for the condition, the appraisal should appraise the net impact on both benefits and costs of the new intervention relative to this benchmark.

NICE also is required to ensure that, in carrying out its statutory functions, it is sympathetic to the longer-term interest of the NHS in encouraging innovation.

Evaluation documentation is prepared by the Appraisals Secretariat or commissioned from expert groups (working closely with the Health Technology Assessment arm of the National Research and Development Programme). An Appraisals Committee (Figure 4.3) carries out the appraisals.

Chairman: Professor David Barnett

Membership

Vice-chair	×1	Hospital physicians	×2
Community nurse	×1	Pharmaceutical physician	×1
Health economists	×3	Surgeon	×1
Pharmacist	×1	Diagnostic pathologist	×1
Biostatistician	×1	General practitioners	×2
Patient advocates	×2	Public health physician	×1
Health managers	×3	Hospital nurse	×1

Additional *ad hoc* members may be appointed 'for the day' by either the Chairman, the Vice-chair, or the Chief Executive

Figure 4.3 Composition of the Appraisal Committee.

NICE produces guidance to commissioners and clinicians on the appropriate use of the intervention alongside current best practice. This guidance covers:

- an assessment of whether or not the intervention can be recommended as clinically effective and as a cost-effective use of NHS resources for NHS use, either in general or in particular circumstances (first- or second-line treatment, for particular subgroups, for routine use or only in the context of targeted research where appropriate, any priorities for treatment)

- recommendations on any questions requiring further research to inform clinical practice, etc.

- an assessment of any wider implications for the NHS

- a concise summary of the reasoning behind NICE's recommendations and the evidence considered.

NICE also prepares guidance for users and carers, consulting with appropriate patient groups on the best format and means of dissemination. This guidance explains the nature of the clinical recommendations, the implications for the standards which patients can expect, and the broad nature of the evidence on which the recommendations are based.

Work programme

The Department of Health formally announced the first and second waves of technologies for NICE to appraise (Boxes 4.1 and 4.2). It has recently announced the third wave that concentrates on cancer drugs: these are Gemcitabine for pancreatic cancer, Temozolamide for brain tumours, Fludarabine and Rituximab for lymphoma, Irinotecan, Oxaliplatin and Raltitrexed for colorectal cancer, Vinorelbine and Gemcitabine for lung cancer, Trastuzumab and Vinorelbine for breast cancer and Topotecan for ovarian cancer. The fourth wave of appraisals will be announced soon.

Box 4.1: Technologies to be appraised (Autumn 1999)

- Hip prosthesis

- Advances in hearing aids

- Routine wisdom teeth extraction

- Liquid based cytology

- Coronary stent developments

- Taxanes for ovarian and breast cancer

- Inhaler systems for childhood asthma (devices)

- PPIs for treatment of dyspepsia

- Beta interferon/glatirimer for multiple sclerosis

- Zanamivir/Oseltamivir for influenza.

Box 4.2: Technologies to be appraised (early 2000)

- Oseltamivir for influenza

- Laparoscopic surgery

- Wound care

- Implantable cardioverter defibrillators

- Autologous cartilage transplantation

- Riluzole for motor neuron disease

- Ritalin for hyperactivity

- Ribavirin/alpha interferon for hepatitis C

- Cyclo-oxygenase II inhibitors for rheumatoid arthritis

- Orlistat and Sibutramine for obesity

- Glitazones for type II diabetes

- Glycoprotein IIb/IIIa receptor inhibitors

- New pharmaceuticals for Alzheimer's disease.

Clinical guidelines

The Institute is also charged with developing and disseminating 'robust and authoritative' clinical guidelines. In constructing its clinical guidelines, the Institute is expected to take into account both clinical and cost effectiveness. Where relevant, the Institute seeks to produce parallel clinical guidelines for patients and their carers.

Key principles

Ten *key principles* will underpin the way in which the Institute handles clinical guideline developments on behalf of the NHS. While there will be many differences between the different kinds of clinical guidelines produced by the Institute, the key principles should be relevant to our approach to all clinical guideline developments.

1 The objective of clinical guidelines is to improve the quality of clinical care by making available to health professionals and patients well-founded advice on best practice.

2 Quality care is based on clinical effectiveness – the extent to which the health status of patients can be expected to be enhanced by clinical interventions.

3 Quality of care in the NHS necessarily includes giving due attention to the cost effectiveness of healthcare interventions.

4 NHS clinical guidelines are relevant to the care provided by the NHS throughout the NHS in England and Wales.

5 NHS clinical guidelines are *advisory*.

6 NHS clinical guidelines are based on the best possible research evidence, expert opinion and professional consensus.

7 NHS clinical guidelines are developed using methods that command the respect of patients, the NHS and NHS stakeholders.

8 While clinical guidelines are focused around the clinical care provided by clinicians, patients are to be treated as full and equal partners along with the relevant professional groups involved in a clinical guideline development.

9 All those who might be affected by a clinical guideline deserve consideration within the clinical guideline development (usually including clinicians, patients and their carers, service managers, the wider public, government and the healthcare industries).

10 NHS clinical guidelines should be both ambitious and realistic in nature. They should set out the clinical care that might reasonably be expected throughout the NHS.

The methodology that the Institute will use to commission its guidelines has been finalised and is on the website. Its current workload is presented in Box 4.3.

Box 4.3: Clinical guidelines to complete or commission

- Management of schizophrenia
- Prevention and treatment of pressure sores
- National cancer group programme
- Peptic ulcer and dyspepsia
- Depressive illness in the community
- Acute myocardial infarction
- Management of completed myocardial infarction in primary care
- Hypertension
- Multiple sclerosis
- Routine pre-operative investigations
- Non-insulin dependent diabetes.

Referral advice

One of the key reasons for the establishment of NICE was to reduce variation in the quality of care provided by the NHS. Variation of the quality of care can be manifested in many ways and one important area is access from primary care into specialist centres. There is now considerable research describing the variability in general practitioner outpatient referral rates, but less understanding on what the underlying reasons are. Key to an effective and efficient health service is the appropriate and timely referral of those patients who will benefit from specialist intervention. In October 1999 the Department of Health and the National Assembly for Wales invited NICE, in addition to its other programmes, to produce an initial set of outpatient referral advice (*see* Box 4.4). These would offer advice to general practitioners on when to refer patients to specialists. The guidance was to be available by April 2000 and a range of topics were proposed.

Box 4.4: Referral advice

• Atopic eczema in children

• Acne

• Psoriasis

• Acute low back pain

• Osteoarthritis of the hip

• Osteoarthritis of the knee

• Glue ear in children

• Recurrent episodes of acute sore throat in children

• Dyspepsia

• Varicose veins

• Urinary tract (outflow) symptoms

• Menorrhagia.

This was a challenging timetable in a field with little research evidence on how this should be approached. Drawing on experience of developing local protocols in South Thames Region and Newcastle, a methodology was designed that adhered to the Institute's generic principals of rigor, transparency and inclusion of all stakeholders.

A steering group was convened to oversee the project. Advisory groups were created to modify and adapt advice created by the NICE project team. Each group consisted of general practitioners, specialists, and patient advocates. These documents are designed to provide advice on when patients should be referred. They are not clinical guidelines on how to manage patients. In the future when the Institute's guidelines programme is established all of its clinical guidelines will include 'referral advice'. This guidance is currently being piloted nationally and will be rolled out to all Primary Care Groups during 2001.

Other NICE initiatives

In addition to these two main strands of work the Institute has also taken over responsibility for supporting clinical audit in the NHS and a number of major programmes, for example, the National Confidential Enquiries and PRODIGY computer support system. These are going through a process of review and policies for their future working patterns are being developed.

The relationship between NICE and the national R&D programme

In describing the interaction it is useful to make a distinction between *research* (as defined within the NHS R&D programme) and *development*. *Research* is defined by process (e.g. its purpose is to create generalisable knowledge) that is protocol based, peer reviewed and will be published. *Development* serves the specific needs of an organisation (like NICE) for information/knowledge/evidence and it does not have to meet the criteria above.

In practice there may be grey areas, for example, an investigation could be undertaken into identifying the most cost-effective strategies for a specific organisation that have some generalisable aspects and therefore have features of *research* although their main intention was *development*. The increasing emphasis on qualitative in addition to quantitative research adds to the requirement to be very specific about the nature of the task being undertaken.

There are three key areas of interaction between the Institute and R&D systems in general and the national R&D programme in particular:

- research and development to enable the Institute to undertake its routine work

- research and development to help the Institute to deliver its work programme more effectively

- the Institute and its products as a subject of research.

In practice these areas will overlap. All areas will involve collation and use of extant research but may also require new research to be initiated. While NICE's routine business involves commissioning research its unique position will also enable the Institute to make a significant contribution to encouraging original research, particularly in the field of methodology.

Research and development to enable the Institute to undertake its routine work

The Institute's appraisals of new and established health technologies as well as its development of its clinical guidelines is inevitably based on the findings of the research community. This takes two forms: the underlying primary research and the secondary systematic reviewing of the available data. The

Institute seeks to foster close relationships with those conducting primary research, and those responsible for its commissioning to ensure that its information needs are satisfied. When it is apparent that further research is needed in the use of a particular technology or the management of a specific condition is to be optimised, the Institute will attempt to describe the area of research need, and indicate by whom it should be conducted.

However, the closest relationship on a routine basis has been with the university departments that undertake the systematic reviews that underpin the appraisal, and the National R&D Health Technology Assessment Programme, through which these are commissioned. Currently these assessments are in the form of 'rapid reviews' and are commissioned via the NCCHTA (National Coordinating Centre for Health Technology Assessment). The current units that have undertaken work for the Institute are based in Southampton, Birmingham, York, Sheffield and Newcastle. The reviews are published in their own right on the HTA website at the same time as the Institute issues its guidance.

There are concerns that the human resources necessary to undertake this expanding role are limited. There are a number of initiatives proposed to ensure that universities value this type of research and create supportive working environments.[4] It is important that university funding bodies are aware of the importance of the NICE research agenda. One idea currently being explored is to second people in/out of NICE to create a cohort of researchers that understand the academic and service issues of NICE's work. There is an urgent need to create proper career paths for these individuals and to prevent a destructive internal market. Within the Institute's appraisal directorate to ensure that staff have academic support, appointments are joint with collaborating universities. At present there are links with York, Brunel and St Georges Hospital Medical School. Staff are encouraged to develop their own research programme linked to NICE's main spheres of activity.

The underlying systematic reviews for the guideline programme will need similar expertise. There are currently very productive discussions between the Department of Health, the R&D directorate and NICE in order to identify what are likely to be the most cost-effective models. Currently, the Institute has inherited a 'professional' model with 'academic' support, and will be working with newly established 'Collaborating Centres'. This approach will be reviewed and modified if necessary over the next 3 years.

NICE is a new organisation and is developing its methods of working daily. While many aspects of the Institute's routine activities depend on established managerial systems and standard project management methods, many aspects have very distinctive features and will need to be evaluated empirically. Discussions have taken place with the methodological section of the R&D programme to identify these needs more carefully.

Research and development to help the Institute to deliver its work programme more effectively

While NICE has some unique features, its main function of technology appraisal is not new and many international institutions are facing the same challenge. There have been a number of informal meetings with similar organisations, but in late 1999 NICE commissioned an international survey of similar institutions to NICE. The results will be published separately, but in summary there is likely to be great scope for sharing many aspects of individual HTA programmes, for example sharing the underlying systematic reviews although the final decision-making processes will be unique to each country.

A key collaboration is being developed with the R&D programme through its Organisational Research Programme.

This is organised by the National Coordinating Centre based in the London School of Hygiene and Tropical Medicine and led by Sir John Pattison. The head of the Guidelines and Audit Programme at NICE has been invited to be on their commissioning committee. This is just commencing but its emphasis on appropriate NHS structures and organisation to bring about improvement in quality is likely to be very pertinent to NICE. The links between the two need to be clarified and the most cost-effective models defined, tested and implemented.

Officially NICE has responsibility for the development and dissemination of its guidance and not implementation; however, unless its guidance is implemented NICE will have deemed to have failed. While there is a substantial research base on ways of maximising guideline implementation, further work is needed particularly in the light of some of the Institute's unique features. The Department of Health, and the R&D programme are working with NICE to develop an ongoing research evaluation programme to identify ways of maximising the likelihood of effective implementation.

The Institute's referral practice booklet is currently being piloted and the London office of the R&D has commissioned an evaluation of its impact on local Primary Care Groups. This provides an early example of how collaboration between key stakeholders at an early stage can ensure that realistic expectations are created.

The basis of NICE's appraisal is the underlying systematic review. To date this has relied heavily on information derived from randomised controlled trials. While this will continue to be considered the 'gold standard' for many evaluations, a number of the interventions assessed by the Institute do not lend themselves to being assessed in this way. Preliminary work suggests that observational studies have a role to play[5,6] and further methodological research in this area is urgently required.

The Institute as a subject of research itself

The formative assessment of the impact of NICE guidance and the identification of the predictors of success has been referred to above. There are, however, many other individuals and organisations keen to research how NICE works, how its committees make their decisions and how its stakeholders respond to the guidance. NICE is currently identifying ways of allowing researchers to have access to the decision-making process without effecting the difficult deliberations that are undertaken in very sensitive and often emotionally charged atmospheres.

Conclusions and managing the tensions

'Synergy' is the latest addition to managerial jargon in the NHS. Defined by the shorter Oxford dictionary as: *the interaction or co-operation of two or more organisations to produce a combined effect greater than the sum of their separate effects*, it can be difficult to achieve in practice. However, in the context of the relationship between NICE and the national R&D programme it is a day-to-day reality. The UK HTA programme as in other countries, has often expressed frustrations that its output did not readily impinge on the consciousness of managers at a local level and policy makers at a national level. This was a problem common to HTA programmes internationally. On the other side the NHS was equally frustrated that the products of R&D were not readily accessible to them. A recent UK and US working party commissioned by the Millbank Memorial Fund[7] highlighted what and how purchasers of healthcare wanted their information. The establishment of NICE should mean that many of these concerns are being tackled.

NICE represents the interface between R&D professional groups and healthcare managers and clinicians, between government and the policy makers and the public and patients. It is a delicate balance to marry aspirational tendencies that we are all subject to with the pragmatism expected of those delivering healthcare to patients on a day-to-day basis. Whether NICE can resolve the differences between a service delivery and research paradigm, only time will tell. No one doubts the challenges facing an NHS organisation working in this field.[8] The pitfalls are frequent and significant. To manage this process and in recognition of its importance the NICE Board agreed at its May 2000 meeting to establish an R&D subcommittee (its first) under the chairmanship of Professor Tony Culyer. This committee will ensure that R&D continues to play a key role in the Institute's day-to-day work as well as mapping out a more strategic future path and its relationship with other organisations. Key organisations responsible for the major R&D activities described in this chapter will be invited to be members to ensure that the Institute maximises its contribution to the R&D efforts already in place.

References

1 Department of Health (1997) *The New NHS: modern, dependable*. HMSO, London.
2 Department of Health (1998) *A First Class Service: quality in the new NHS*. HMSO, London.
3 Rawlins M (1999) In pursuit of quality: the National Institute for Clinical Excellence. *Lancet*. **353**:1079–82.
4 Frenk J (1992) Balancing relevance and excellence: organizational responses to link research with decision making. *Soc Sci Med*. **35**(11):1397–404.
5 Benson K and Hartz AJ (2000) A comparison of observational studies and randomised controlled trials. *NEJM*. **442**(25):1878–84.

6 Concato J, Shah N and Horwitz R (2000) Randomised controlled trials, observational studies, and the hierarchy of research designs. *NEJM*. **342**(25):1887–92.
7 *Better Information, Better Outcomes? The use of Health Technology Information and Clinical Data in Health Care Purchasing decisions in the United Kingdom and the United States*. Millbank Memorial Fund 2000, New York.
8 Swales JD (2000) Science and health care: an uneasy partnership. *Lancet*. **355**:1637–40.

5

Funding NHS R&D: implementing Culyer

CLIFF BAILEY

The NHS R&D funding scheme for England was established in 1997. Recommendations made by Professor Anthony Culyer in his report, *Supporting Research and Development in the NHS* in 1994[1] suggested that funding for R&D be separated from funding provided for patient care and an R&D budget be established. The budget was provided by consolidating into a single budget all of the funding streams previously provided for the purchase of research by the Department of Health, and adding to this money raised by a levy on all NHS providers housing research. The providers were asked to identify and declare the costs incurred by them in housing the research; this amount of money was then deducted from their overall allocations and added to the R&D budget. The budget was then divided into two parts: one to fund work commissioned by a central programme, and the second to be returned to NHS providers to provide the support costs for the research which they house (*see* Figure 5.1). Funding was to be returned to the providers following a bidding process in which they identified the necessary infrastructural costs to house the research and the research areas against which the funding was to be allocated.

Bids were assessed first by teams in each of the regional offices and were then subjected to a central cross-reading

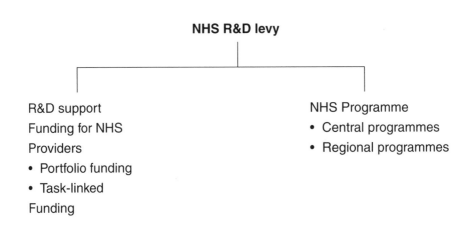

Figure 5.1 The NHS R&D budget.

stage. In the judgement of the bids it was decided that it was not possible to make an assessment of the scientific quality of each individual research project. The teams instead assessed the bids against ten dimensions of assessment. These included a judgement of the systems which providers had in place to internally assess the quality of research projects supported from their possible R&D allocation, judgement of their R&D management systems and judgement of the arrangements in place to ensure that all research met agreed ethical standards. The assessment teams also sought evidence in the bids of the existence of academic partnership, of multi-disciplinary research activity, of consumer involvement in the research activity and of the involvement of other healthcare sectors such as primary care (*see* Box 5.1).

NHS providers could elect to either bid for funding on their own account or in partnership with other providers where such a consortium would provide a greater breadth of coherent research activity than would otherwise be the case. Those providers with higher levels of research activity, who were able to absorb the small swings in funding caused by the start up of new projects, and the completion of others within a stable amount of funding, could opt for a type of contract

---

Box 5.1: Dimensions of assessment

- Quality

- Strategic ability

- Partnership

- Management

- Costs

- Multi-disciplinary involvement

- Consumer involvement

- Ethics

- Primary care involvement

- Relevance to the NHS.

---

which would provide an agreed income for 3 years and would allow the provider the right to vire money between research activity areas. These were called portfolio contracts. Those providers who felt unable to absorb the risk of fluctuating research costs against fixed income were able to bid for a contract, called a task-linked contract, for between 1 and 4 years. They would therefore be able to re-bid in the event of significant fluctuation in the level of research activity. Virement between activity areas in this type of contract was only allowed after discussion with the regional office. In order to allow for in-year cash adjustment when significant fluctuation did occur, an *ad hoc* fund was established open to those with task-linked contracts.

Research activity in NHS providers fell into three main categories:

- research funded by an external, non-commercial agency

- research funded by commercial agencies

- un-funded research.

The first of these categories included the research conducted in the NHS on behalf of the research councils. Agreement to provide funding to enable NHS providers to house this work was contained in the concordat between the NHS and the research councils. The NHS R&D directorate took the view that, whilst no formal concordat existed, it wished to provide similar support to the work of the major health-related charities which provided research funding for work conducted in the NHS. The criterion adopted was that the work should be quality assured by the provision by the funder of an external peer review system. Providers were asked to identify their costs associated with this peer reviewed, externally funded, non-commercial work and these costs were accepted as a first call on the budget.

The assessment teams were only able to make judgements around the claimed involvement, or otherwise, of the NHS provider in the study. There was no method by which they could verify either the cost claimed or the claimed quantum of involvement in the study. This gave rise to particular difficulties with multi-centre trials, where one centre may have provided leadership and co-ordination of the study, whilst others contributed patients and incurred costs in managing those patients and yet others contributed patients who received the study intervention in another centre at no cost to themselves.

Commercially funded R&D also posed some difficulties of interpretation for the assessment teams. There were two forms of work in this category. The first was work funded by a commercial organisation, the results of which were to be used for its own benefit, for example, for licensing purposes for new pharmaceuticals. The service was instructed that this type of work was to be charged at full costs to the industry, and was therefore not an allowable cost against the R&D budget.

The second category was when a piece of research was funded by a commercial agency, but the results of the research were 'for the public benefit'. This proved difficult to define in practice, leaving regional research directors to make judgements on a case-by-case basis.

The third category of research activity was work being undertaken without any external funding support, and it was in this area that the greatest difficulties were encountered by the assessment teams. Despite a considerable amount of explanation to those in the service responsible for submission of individual bids, that the new scheme did not represent a new source of project funding, the bids contained a large amount of requests for this type of funding. As a result, the amount of money initially bid for far exceeded the amount of money in the budget. Whilst the bid documents asked providers to detail the quality control systems used to monitor work carried out on their premises, it was often not clear to the assessment teams how, or if, these systems had been applied to the work for which they were seeking support. There were approximately 20 000 projects in this category reported by the providers to the National Research Register (NRR). It was therefore impossible to ensure that every one was being conducted to a properly written, peer-reviewed protocol. It is certain that there was an enormous range in the quality of the work supported under this heading. The work was largely driven by the individual interests and enthusiasms of researchers and encompassed a wide subject area without any reference to areas of research priority.

In arriving at judgements about the allocations to be made, the assessment teams had to first ensure that the provider had satisfied them that they met the standards required on the ten dimensions of assessment. They then had to ensure that the externally funded, peer-reviewed work was supported. The un-funded work then had to be sifted and judgements made as to its quality and relevance and as to whether the bid reflected work truly in progress or whether it was an aspirational bid to fund new work.

Each NHS region was then given a notional budget based on the amount of money identified by that region as its contribution to the central budget. The regional directors and their teams indicated to the national director of R&D how, in their view, the national budget should be allocated to providers in their region. Small movements of funding were thus made possible within regions. However, little could be done to move larger amounts of funding between regions. The funding was not subject to any targeting towards priority areas of research, and neither was it possible to shift significant amounts of money between healthcare sectors. In particular, primary care, as a sector towards which there was a desire to move funding, could not be as well supported as might have been ideal.

Box 5.2: Time-limited national programmes

- Mental health/learning disabilities

- Cardiovascular disease/stroke

- Cancer

- Mother and child health

- Asthma

- Physical and complex disabilities

- Primary/secondary care interface

- Implementation

- Primary dental care.

The central programme consisted of the Health Technology Assessment (HTA) programme, the eight regional programmes and a series of time-limited, subject-specific commissioned research programmes (*see* Box 5.2). It was decided that, as each of the time-limited programmes drew towards its completion, it should be discontinued. The cash thus released should be utilised to continue the HTA programme and create two new national programmes, the Service Delivery and

Organisation programme (SDO) and the New and Emerging Applications of Technology programme (NEAT).

In 1999, Professor Michael Clarke was commissioned by the Central Research and Development Committee to undertake a review of the NHS R&D levy.[2] He also undertook to advise on the strategic decisions implicit in the allocation process. He noted: 'In the few years since the Research and Development programme has been established, every region and major hospital has research and development managed with explicit research and training programmes, and plans for future development. Achieving these changes is something of which the NHS can be justifiably proud.' Regional Directors of R&D, whilst having to manage the disappointment of some providers who had large aspirations, which could not be fulfilled, have, none-the-less, noted an enthusiasm for research and research awareness spreading through the service. Clarke identified four main areas for renewed effort:

- a clearer focus on NHS needs and priorities
- improved quality assurance systems for research programmes
- the systematic involvement of wider health communities and consumers in NHS research and development
- the development of research capacity in terms of research training and career prospects.

The first of these areas requires consideration to be given to the fact that NHS funding is but one contribution to the overall health-related research field. The academic infrastructure is provided by the Higher Education Funding Council for England (HEFCE). Considerable amounts of basic and clinical research are provided by the research councils and by major charities. As well as ensuring access to the NHS for research provided by others, the Department of Health (DoH) itself also funds a sizeable research portfolio. It is essential that

the DoH works with these partners, to clarify the contribution to be made by each, and that the DoH takes a leading
role in health services research. Clarke recommended that a
rolling programme of reviews be established to inform
strategic priorities for research. Accurate information as to
research in progress is clearly necessary to inform programme
planners of progress or otherwise against these strategic
priorities. The NRR exists as a tool to deliver this information.
In its early stages of development the NRR attracted criticism
because the data held was incomplete and repetitive. Considerable efforts have now been made to improve the data set
and completeness and accuracy of input is now a contractual
requirement of those receiving funding from the NHS R&D
budget. Thus, whilst further effort will undoubtedly be
needed to maintain and further improve the standard of data
in the future, the NRR should become an increasingly
valuable resource.

In order to inform the group led by Professor Clarke,
ministers established five topic working groups to advise on
future needs for health-related research in priority areas. The
five groups were established in the areas of ageing, cancer,
mental health, cardiovascular disease and stroke, and primary
care. The groups did valuable work in a short time period
to provide a snapshot of the state of the art at that time,
and made some helpful recommendations. Professor Clarke
recommended that time-limited national research advisory
groups in research priority areas be established in order to
foster relevant comprehensive research across all constituent
health communities. Three such groups have now been established in cancer, cardiovascular disease and stroke, and in
mental health.

In addressing the issue of quality assurance, Professor
Clarke noted that the R&D programme supported upwards of
20 000 projects to a value of £420m. £350m of this is accounted
for by support funding for NHS providers. As noted above
some of this money supports projects subjected to stringent

quality control through the external peer review systems of the research councils, the major charities and the NHS programme itself. However, two-thirds of this funding supports work initiated and managed by the providers themselves, with, as noted above, variable quality control systems. Clarke considered that all such support funding should be subject to the highest level of peer review but pointed out that to do so for such a large number of individual projects was impractical. Instead he suggested the reorganisation of the funding mechanisms towards the creation of a number of research programmes and centres. He considered that this could bring about the following improvements:

- a regular review system

- greater emphasis being placed on research on priority areas

- the involvement of wider health communities in the research process.

Involvement of wider health communities would reflect close co-operation between NHS providers and relevant academic units in order to underpin the quality of research funded by the levy. It would also imply that in creating a research programme or centre, attention should be given to the constituent parts of the programme. It would involve a range of research activity from basic scientific through to social research issues, a range of research methodologies, and therefore a range of different types of NHS provider and co-operation from relevant providers in other fields such as social services, education and housing. It would be anticipated that such programmes would attract funding from HEFCE through the higher education provider, the Medical and the Economic and Social Sciences Research Councils and from the NHS R&D budget.

Building greater research capacity and paying particular attention to areas of identified skills shortage was identified by Clarke as a key priority for future development of the R&D programme. This is not an area which the DoH is capable of addressing without the co-operation of others, particularly HEFCE and the research councils. The NHS R&D programme has now established a cross-cutting portfolio of work in this field, which is working closely with the above to ensure that appropriate training opportunities are provided. It is exploring how trainees can be provided with clear career pathways and secure long-term career opportunities.

In March 2000 the DoH published a document *Research and Development for a First Class Service: R&D funding in the new NHS*[3] in which it set out the policy context and described the development programme for the management of NHS R&D funding in England. The document describes how a transition will be achieved in the structure of the NHS R&D budget over the next 5 years in order that it can better address some of the lessons learned from the first 3 years of operation, and some of the issues raised by Clarke (*see* Figure 5.2).

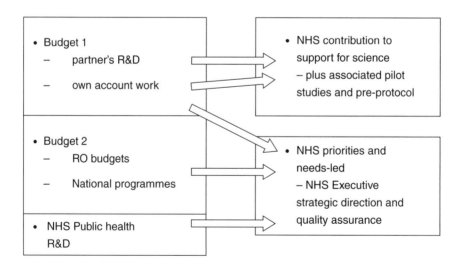

Figure 5.2 The structure of the NHS R&D budget over the next 5 years.

The NHS R&D budget must continue to support the high-quality work done in the NHS by the Research Councils and the major research charities. It will do this by creating a funding system to be called NHS Support for Science. The exact mechanisms by which this will operate are, at the time of writing, subject to a consultation exercise before they can be finalised. It is likely to involve the better development of partnership agreements between the DoH and those research funders who wish to use the NHS as a test bed in which to conduct their research. In exchange for access to service support funding for their work, partners are likely to be asked to share their research strategy with the DoH. They should be able to demonstrate the existence of external peer review mechanisms for quality control, and to be able to demonstrate a degree of open access to any funding which they offer. They will be invited to work with the DoH to develop reference costs to be applied in arriving at a quantum of service support costs associated with their studies, and to allow some form of cross-referencing between their records and those of the NHS provider regarding the quantum of involvement of a particular provider in a study.

The scheme will recognise that the development of new research ideas and protocols is a time-consuming activity that needs to be encouraged by the provision of an amount of funding. Service providers who can show that they have within the institution a number of principal investigators for studies will qualify to have a percentage added to their support for science allowance to recognise this added commitment.

Allowances will then be computed by taking verified involvement in a recognised study and multiplying the quantum of involvement by the agreed reference cost. The amounts for each study will be accumulated and the principal investigator allowance added. Providers will then receive the allocation on an annual basis in line with other NHS funding arrangements.

The remainder of the NHS R&D budget will form the second source of funding to be called the Priorities and Needs Fund. At present the money in this fund is supporting the work in providers not funded by external partners and the national and regional programmes. The creation of this single stream will in the first instance allow the expenditure to be more directed towards addressing the priorities for research identified by the DoH. It will be possible to introduce coherence between the previously non-coherent parts of the DoH R&D programme and to encourage NHS providers to channel their research efforts towards priority subjects. In the future it is envisaged that funding in this scheme will move away from funding individual providers. Instead it will move towards funding a number of research centres and programmes which whilst involving individual providers will also involve a number of other partners.

A number of models will need to be considered for the creation of these research centres. In any model an essential component will be a close association with relevant academic units who will provide academic rigour to the research programme. This will represent an opportunity and a challenge to academic units. On the one hand they will be presented with the opportunity to work closely with academically orientated service providers and have access to the facility of the NHS, whilst on the other hand they will be required to provide support to a wider range of individuals than was previously the case. They will argue that the funding which they receive from HEFCE will not allow them to do this and will worry that to do so might dilute their research effort detracting from their performance in the research assessment exercise (RAE) used to determine this funding. The DoH has established a strategic alliance with HEFCE to ensure that these issues are addressed and suitable agreed solutions are found. DoH representatives will sit on each of the relevant assessment panels in the forthcoming RAE. Three joint task forces have met to consider the relationship between the RAE and various aspects of the service. Task forces 1 and 2 have published their findings and task force 3, which is considering aspects of research particular to the nursing, midwifery and health visiting professions as well as research in the professions allied to medicine, continues to meet. It may be necessary to negotiate contracts or to renegotiate existing contracts with academic units to ensure that they have the resource necessary to provide support to the NHS research centres as well as ensuring that they have the full support of HEFCE and their host institutions.

Service providers could be brought together to form research centres in a number of ways. One model might be for a number of providers in a related field to agree to work together with appropriate academic support to form a research centre. An example might be a number of mental health providers each individually relatively small in research terms but together achieving critical mass. Another model might be the placing of a research centre in a service provider already recognised as a centre in terms of service delivery for a national service framework and requiring that the centre create relationships with its local academic centre as well as with a managed clinical network of service providers in its geographic region. An example of this model might be found in the Calman–Hine arrangement for cancer service delivery. A third model might be the creation of a virtual centre composed of an academic unit on, for instance, cardiovascular disease, associated with the cardiovascular providers in tertiary, secondary and primary care and with representatives from community and social care. Such a centre would be able to assemble a wide range of expertise and would be able to support a broad research portfolio.

Funding for such centres would consist of core funding provided to support the infrastructure of the centre from HEFCE for the academic components and complementary funding from NHS R&D for the service components. Centres would be able to attract programme funding from NHS R&D

for work in NHS priority areas and from other programme funders such as the research councils. Project funding would be available from all of the usual external funding sources as well as from the HTA, SDO and NEAT programmes and NHS regional programmes.

References

1 Culyer A (1994) *Supporting Research and Development in the NHS*. HMSO, London.
2 *Strategic Review of the NHS R&D Levy*. A report to the Central Research and Development Committee (1999).
3 Department of Health (2000) *Research and Development for a First Class Service: R&D funding in the new NHS*. Department of Health, London.

6

Information for R&D

JOS KLEIJNEN

Background

Good decisions about health and social care rely on a number of factors such as priorities, needs, resources and systematic reviews of the results of research. R&D for NHS priorities and needs provides such systematic reviews as well as the primary research which is summarised in these reviews. This information can be about clinical topics such as the diagnosis and treatment of disease; about the provision and organisation of health and related social care; about public health and health services and, finally, about quality assurance. Basic and strategic research is not a main part of R&D but it further informs decisions, be it from a greater distance. More importantly, it stimulates and supports both the initiation and interpretation of R&D research.

Research is a circular process, starting with the generation of hypotheses. These are informed by systematic reviews from previous basic, strategic and clinical research. New research is initiated to test such hypotheses and the findings are then incorporated in new, updated systematic reviews, which should also take into account information from other new research that has become available in the meantime. Then new hypotheses can be developed and the process starts again.

There is a great deal of R&D research being performed and even more is already available. It makes sense to make good use of what we already know and to prevent unnecessary duplication of precious research efforts. This applies to local, national and international levels. Fortunately, in the 21st century, it is easier than in the past to make information quickly and widely available using modern media such as the World Wide Web.

What information is needed for R&D, and who needs it?

There are many types of information that are useful for R&D. These include demographic/epidemiological information, aetiological, diagnostic and prognostic information and, usually most important for R&D, therapeutic and economic information. However, diagnostic information is currently given more emphasis than some time ago, and rightfully so. In terms of using R&D for good decisions, process and outcomes information are also important.

Demographic, epidemiological, aetiological and prognostic information help in the prioritisation of diagnostic and therapeutic research. Whereas there are nowadays, in the time of evidence-based healthcare, many sources of information that already have been appraised for their validity and usefulness for practice, these tend to focus on diagnostic and therapeutic information.

Patients, healthcare professionals, providers and politicians need information (usually diagnostic, therapeutic or service delivery and organisation information) that would help them in making decisions about healthcare. If the information that is needed is not available, R&D may be able to provide it, if good prioritisation processes for research are in place. Researchers and those funding research also need information to help them formulate the hypotheses and objectives for research. All types of information may be relevant for formulation of objectives for research. The best resource of information for decision making is systematic reviews. These should be the first choice to answer questions about clinical effectiveness. By systematically searching, assessing and summarising the research evidence, systematic reviews present a time-saving distillation of the current state of knowledge.[1]

Sources of information

Information about healthcare is traditionally reported in healthcare journals and other publications. The amount of this information is daunting, and impossible to digest. Therefore, for many decades, this information is being catalogued in information retrieval systems. These were traditionally big paper volumes, for example *Index Medicus* and *Excerpta Medica*, and since the availability of computers big databases that can be searched on-line or on CD-ROM, such as *Medline* and *Embase*. There are nowadays many such databases, which provide titles, abstracts and source information about papers published in journals; readers are referred to their library to see what is available. Except for therapeutic and economic information, these databases are usually the first step in the search for information. The World Wide Web is gradually becoming the most important source of information, and also makes the other sources better and more conveniently accessible.

The information is produced by researchers who get their funding from government, funding agencies, charities and industry. The NHS R&D programme funds various programmes and groups to produce research that informs decision making in the NHS. Each of the NHS R&D programmes have their own websites which include further details about currently ongoing research. An overview is available on: http://www.doh.gov.uk/research/index.htm. Examples would be the Health Technology Assessment Programme (http://www.hta.nhsweb.nhs.uk/), the Service Delivery and Organisation Programme (http://www.sdo.lshtm.ac.uk/), entities of the Cochrane Collaboration (http://www.cochrane.de/), and the NHS Centre for Reviews and Dissemination (http://www.york.ac.uk/inst/crd/). The National Institute for Clinical Excellence (NICE – also *see* below) works together with these groups and programmes in order to prepare guidance and guidelines and to assess the evidence for new interventions for the NHS (http://www.nice.org.uk/nice-web/). NICE also uses information provided by industry.

Each NHS Regional Office has an R&D Directorate. Regional Offices work within the context of developments in national R&D policy. They identify R&D priorities for the region; fund R&D activities of value to the NHS; develop R&D capacity across the region, including primary care; and, finally, they disseminate information about R&D findings and promote an evaluative culture. Links to all regional R&D offices are available: http://www.doh.gov.uk/research/rd3/regions.htm.

Ongoing research

All ongoing and recently completed research projects funded by, or of interest to, the United Kingdom's National Health Service are available in a register: *The National Research Register* (NRR). It contains information on just under 64 000 research projects, as well as entries from the Medical Research Council's Clinical Trials Register, and details on reviews in progress collected by the NHS Centre for Reviews and Dissemination. The NRR is assembled and published by Update Software Ltd on behalf of the Department of Health in the UK. The register is available on: http://www.update-software.com/. The NRR can be used to identify unpublished research, to provide early warning on research which may lead to important findings, to help avoid unnecessary duplication in research and to help improve the uptake and participation in research.

Current Controlled Trials contains the metaRegister of Controlled Trials (mRCT), which is a 'register of registers' of ongoing controlled trials. It searches the indexes to a number of trials registers including the Alzheimer's Disease Society, the British Heart Foundation, the Clinical Trial Service Unit, the Medical Research Council, the National Institutes of Health and many more, and is available on: http://www.controlled-trials.com/.

www.clinicaltrials.gov contains records of over 4000 trials sponsored mainly by the US National Institutes for Health. It also includes trials funded by other federal agencies, the pharmaceutical industry and non-profit organisations. It is mainly aimed at the public, but contains lots of descriptive information and links to other pages.

The Cochrane Library (*see* below) provides protocols of ongoing systematic reviews. In addition to general information about ongoing research, there are also more topic specific websites about ongoing projects, for example about cancer. Some of these are described on the following websites from the NHS Centre for Reviews and Dissemination: http://www.york.ac.uk/inst/crd/htadbase.htm.

Health Technology Assessment Databases

There are several Health Technology Assessment Databases. One example is the *Health Technology Assessment (HTA) Database*, produced by the NHS Centre for Reviews and Dissemination in collaboration with the secretariat of the

International Network of Agencies for Health Technology Assessment (INAHTA http://www.inahta.org/). This database contains details of HTA publications and ongoing HTA projects. This database is available on: http://agatha.york. ac.uk/welcome.htm and also in the Cochrane Library (*see* below). Another example is the US National Library of Medicine's Health Services/Technology Assessment Text (HSTAT) at http://text.nlm.nih.gov. HSTAT is a free, electronic resource that provides access to the full text of documents useful in healthcare decision making.

Information that has been critically appraised

The Cochrane Library is an electronic publication designed to supply high quality evidence to inform people providing and receiving care, and those responsible for research, teaching, funding and administration at all levels. It is published quarterly on CD-ROM and the Internet, and is distributed on a subscription basis. Available on: http://www.updatesoftware. com/. The Cochrane Library contains six databases:

1 The *Cochrane Database of Systematic Reviews* (1750 systematic reviews and protocols)

2 The *Database of Abstracts of Reviews of Effectiveness* (1900 abstracts of systematic reviews)

3 The *Cochrane Controlled Trials Register* (290 000 randomised trials)

4 The *Cochrane Methodology Register* (1350 methodology papers)

5 The *Health Technology Assessment Database* (2000 abstracts)

6 The *NHS Economic Evaluation Database* (more than 5600 entries, more than 2000 abstracts).

The *Database of Abstracts of Reviews of Effectiveness* (DARE), the *Health Technology Assessment Database* and the *NHS Economic Evaluation Database* (NHS EED) are also available free on the website of the NHS Centre for Reviews and Dissemination at http://www.york.ac.uk/inst/crd/htadbase.htm. DARE is a database of high quality systematic research reviews of the effectiveness of healthcare interventions. It provides structured abstracts of (non-Cochrane) systematic reviews and provides a discussion of the strengths and weaknesses of these reviews. NHS EED is a database of structured abstracts of economic evaluations of healthcare interventions, and also provides a discussion of the strengths and weaknesses of these economic evaluations.

BMJ Clinical Evidence is a 6-monthly, updated compendium of evidence on the effects of common clinical interventions. It provides a concise account of the current state of the best available evidence about the prevention and treatment of a wide range of clinical conditions based on thorough searches of the literature. Where there is no good evidence, it says so. It is available as a book and also on-line at http://online.clinicalevidence.com/.

Best Evidence is a cumulative, searchable database. It includes *ACP Journal Club* and *Evidence-Based Medicine. ACP Journal Club* and *Evidence-Based Medicine* provide structured abstracts and critical comments about the 2% or so of articles which they deem to be both valid and useful for healthcare professionals. Recently, *ACP Journal Club* was integrated with *Evidence-Based Medicine.*[2]

The government's recent Information Strategy for the NHS announced the intention to introduce a National electronic Library for Health (NeLH) by March 2002. The NeLH is now a programme of work within the portfolio of the NHS Information Authority. The role of the NeLH will be to provide healthcare professionals and the public (through NHS Direct Online and the New Library Network) with knowledge and know-how to support healthcare-related decisions. The

NeLH will: provide easy access to best, current knowledge and know-how; improve health and healthcare, clinical practice and patient choice. The NeLH will be available via NHSnet and the Internet at http://www.nelh.nhs.uk/.

Guidelines and guidance

NICE was set up as a Special Health Authority for England and Wales in 1999. It is part of the NHS and provides patients, health professionals and the public with guidance on current 'best practice'. The guidance covers both individual health technologies (including medicines, medical devices, diagnostic techniques and procedures) and the clinical management of specific conditions (http://www.nice.org.uk/nice-web/).

The Agency for Healthcare Research and Quality research (AHRQ) provides evidence-based information on healthcare outcomes, quality, cost, use, and access. Information from AHRQ's research helps people make more informed decisions and improve the quality of healthcare services. AHRQ was formerly known as the Agency for Health Care Policy and Research (http://www.ahrq.gov/). The AHRQ's website provides a good entry to US information for R&D, including a link to the National Guideline Clearinghouse (NGC), a public resource for evidence-based clinical practice guidelines at: http://www.guideline.gov/index.asp.

Other information

The *Research Findings electronic Register* (ReFeR) at http://www.doh.gov.uk/research/rd3/information/findings.htm is a freely available database, providing 'prompt sight' of the findings of completed research from the NHS R&D Programme and the DoH Policy Research Programme. ReFeR contains summaries of research findings from single 'primary' research studies as well as systematic reviews of primary studies.

The *Turning Research into Practice* (TRIP) database is an amalgamation of 26 databases of hyperlinks from 'evidence-based' sites around the world. At present there are over 10 000 links to evidence-based topics, so TRIP provides a simple search mechanism and is available at http://www.ceres.uwcm.ac.uk/.

Discussion

In 1999, the British government published a public health policy document, a White Paper *Saving Lives: our healthier nation*. To help those responsible for implementing the proposed policies, contributors to the Cochrane Collaboration and the Campbell Collaboration (http://campbell.gse.upenn.edu) and staff from the NHS Centre for Reviews and Dissemination have prepared a substantial document called 'Evidence from systematic reviews of research relevant to implementing the "wider public health" agenda'.[3] The document is available free at http://www.york.ac.uk/inst/crd/wph.htm. The material in the document follows the classification and listing of over 200 policies set out in the White Paper. It also covers areas of 'the wider public health' which are not included in the White Paper, but which can inform the development of further strategies on education, social care and social welfare, and crime, drugs and alcohol.

In the report nearly 1000 systematic reviews are referenced, of which 400 have been prepared with funding or support from the NHS R&D Programme. The reviews should be helpful in deciding which intended policies might be prioritised, because there is evidence that suggests that they are likely to succeed. In addition, they may help to identify effective interventions and ways of delivering them in order to achieve the policies. Finally the reviews may help to identify further policies, because there is evidence from systematic reviews that certain interventions may improve public health.

This 'Wider Public Health Report' demonstrates that there is not necessarily a big discrepancy between the types of information wanted and needed by decision makers versus those available. Information for R&D and from R&D is widely available, although it may be sometimes difficult to find. The resources cited in this chapter may be a good starting point in the search for useful and valid information.

References

1 Glanville J and Lefebvre C (2000) Identifying systematic reviews: key resources. *Evidence-Based Medicine*. **5**:68–9.
2 *Best Evidence* [CD-ROM] (1999) American College of Physicians – American Society of Internal Medicine, Philadelphia.
3 Contributors to the Cochrane Collaboration and the Campbell Collaboration. Evidence from systematic reviews of research relevant to implementing the 'wider public health' agenda. NHS Centre for Reviews and Dissemination, August 2000.

7

Ethics of clinical and health services research

IAIN J SMITH AND ANTONY FRANKS

Introduction

Ethics, or moral philosophy, is a complex matter. It involves rules, principles and individual circumstances. Judgement mixed with reasoning and emotion, influenced by intuition, guides the decision-making process.

The complexity of human behaviour and the plurality of society make it extremely difficult to develop and implement absolute rules of behaviour. As a result judging the rightness, or otherwise, of decisions is complicated because such rules are, in part, socially determined. In Western biomedical ethics moral philosophers have tended to utilise either of two contrasting moral theories: utilitarianism and deontology. In the former actions are judged on their consequences in terms of maximising happiness or wellbeing; happiness or wellbeing includes the absence of pain or distress. Simply put, the ends justify the means where the ends are deemed to be morally correct. By contrast deontology is duty-based ethics where the means are ends in themselves; the rules governing behaviour are more important than the consequences. For example, truth telling might be deemed to be more important than the outcomes even if the outcomes are undesirable.

Neither moral theory helps in solving difficult problems with respect to individuals or wider society.

Over the past two decades, four derived moral principles of autonomy, beneficence, non-maleficence and justice have been widely utilised. These principles are largely consonant with the two main moral theories (summarised above) and indeed with the beliefs of the major world religions and most cultural groups. These principles are not intended to provide simple solutions to complex ethical problems but are considered to be of value in that they provide not only a common moral language but also a framework for the analysis of complex decisions. The principles are often in conflict; for example, clinical research may cause problems for individuals in terms of their participation but may produce results that would benefit the larger population. The remainder of this chapter will consider some of the difficult ethical problems faced by researchers in their desire to improve not only the care to be offered to individual patients but also the acquisition of knowledge.

In allowing the healthcare professions a degree of licence in their use of treatments, which have not been scientifically validated, society expects there to be ethical safeguards. It is not now acceptable for new treatments to be introduced without collecting evidence of effectiveness, safety and acceptability. The implementation of such evidence-based practice will have two significant consequences in the context of clinical research. The first will be to question the value of existing treatments in terms of clinical effectiveness and acceptability, for example, the use of combined abdominal and vaginal hysterectomy when the latter may be sufficient. The second will be in the introduction of increasingly expensive new drugs to a resource constrained NHS, for example, beta interferon and the management of multiple sclerosis.

Autonomy

In exercising autonomy individuals are able to choose freely a course of action relating to themselves. To exercise such a freedom of choice it is necessary that an individual has sufficient knowledge about the risks and benefits of a particular course of action and they must be able to act without constraint or coercion. The knowledge required is that which will allow him or her to be able to make an appropriate informed choice; it is not necessary to turn the individual into an expert. Healthcare professionals have to recognise that most patients will be exchanging some autonomy for care and while the capacity to make choices may be affected by ill health, disease or physiological disturbance, ultimately only the individual can make the most appropriate choice for themselves.

Linked to the need to preserve, or indeed enhance, autonomy in making choices about participation in clinical research is the reassurance that patients will be treated with respect. This respect includes the need to preserve privacy and confidentiality as well as the reassurance that they are not being coerced and that the truth about risks and benefits is being presented. Information giving, and its understanding, requires that appropriate levels of detail about harm are presented to the individual patient or research subject. Overly complex and detailed patient information sheets are as unacceptable as no information at all.

Beneficence

Beneficence requires that healthcare should maximise the good to be done to and for people. Clinical practice based on research-derived evidence is likely to maximise the benefit of healthcare interventions for both individual people and the wider society. Because clinically effective treatments will more rapidly return individuals to the best state from which they can exercise their own autonomy, the maximisation of beneficence will include the maximisation of autonomy. Historically, clinical research has been bedevilled by medical paternalism; the professionals' belief that they knew what was best for individual patients led to the implicit acceptance that the research subjects' trust in the researcher would be soundly based in the fact that the researcher would only act in the patients' best interests. Increasingly researchers are being encouraged to enter into partnership arrangements with participating patients and to include representative patients in the design phase of research projects; thus the autonomy of patients is respected. This approach, it is argued, will not only increase ownership (and thus commitment) among participating patients but also add value by including research outcomes that matter to individual patients.

Non-maleficence

One of the most important medical rules that is applied to individual patients is that doctors should first do no harm. In research, harm should be minimised by ensuring that the risks and benefits are clearly presented, not only to research ethics committees, but also to individual patients. Moreover, researchers should avoid wasting people's time by conducting research which is either trivial or technically incompetent. Scientifically invalid research is unethical in that it is incapable of providing results of value and diverts scarce resources to no benefit. Participating patients should be assured that the research is important, will be completed and will be published.

Justice

In modern bioethics justice is primarily concerned with the fair distribution of resources and opportunities. The central guiding phrases are derived from Aristotle who indicated that equals should be treated equally and that unequals should be treated equally. This is particularly difficult for researchers who may find that, because of language barriers, some groups in society will not be included in research trials. Difficulties arise in translating consent forms and patient information sheets and consequently a number of ethnic minority groups may be excluded from participation in clinical trials. Therefore, the results of such trials cannot be assumed to be relevant to such groups. This issue is not however restricted to issues of ethnicity; thus the elderly, and women, in whom the majority of heart attacks occur, are poorly represented in most clinical trials of early treatment for heart attacks.

Human clinical research

Clinical research involving human subjects has been widely practised for centuries. Invariably the principal researchers were medical doctors and little attention was paid to seeking consent from research subjects. Indeed, until the middle of the 20th century a significant number of research projects were conducted on vulnerable groups, for example, patients in asylums and children in orphanages. The Nuremberg trials at the end of the Second World War proved to be a turning point in human clinical research. When the extent of Nazi experimentation on prisoners was exposed a set of research principles (the Nuremberg code) was widely accepted. The code holds that experiments should yield fruitful results for the good of society unprocurable by other means; a balance must be reached between societal and individual benefit and the risks to individual participants. The key consequence of this code was that human research could only be conducted on fully informed autonomous individuals. This clearly excluded the very young, the clinically ill and possibly the mentally ill. A number of revisions of the ethical codes for research have been developed; known as the Helsinki codes, the last revisions were made in 1996. The codes now permit clinical research in vulnerable groups who cannot offer their own informed consent only when the risk is minimal and benefits clearly important.

In line with these international codes the NHS has had in place since 1967 a series of ethics committees whose principal purpose was to satisfy themselves on the ethics of research proposals. As a result of a number of national and international directives the purpose and function of these ethics committees has evolved. They are designated as advisory committees and have no statutory functions. This is different from the US where ethics committees were first instituted by formal legislation. Consequently these Institutional Review Boards have extended their remits to include difficult local clinical ethical problems. Thus they exert more direct influence on healthcare professionals both in research and clinical practice than is the case in the UK.

Ethical scrutiny of all research funded by, or carried out in, the NHS is an absolute prerequisite. Currently each health authority has at least one research ethics committee to consider local research proposals. These Local Research Ethics Committees (LRECs) are usually hospital-based and include medical professionals (including general practitioners), nurses and other professions allied to medicine as well as a variable number of lay representatives. These committees meet at variable intervals depending upon the research culture of the health authority and its associated hospitals. Some committees will only meet every three months or so, whilst others may meet bi-weekly. This is usually representative of the volume of research being undertaken locally rather than a lowering of the threshold for ethical scrutiny and so teaching hospital ethics committees are likely to meet more frequently.

A number of researchers and their sponsors have commented unfavourably on the length of time taken to get multiple LREC approval before multicentre clinical studies could be undertaken; in some cases it has taken up to 18 months after the proposal was submitted. Most LRECs also had their own locally produced application forms which added to the administrative burden for the researchers. In 1997 each NHS Regional Office was instructed to set up and run a Multicentre Research Ethics Committee (MREC) to facilitate ethical consideration for multicentre studies. It was intended that this fast-track process would facilitate such studies; approval by MREC meant that LRECs could only consider issues specific to their local setting, not the broader questions of whether the research met ethical requirements. However, a review of the time taken to institute such studies has failed to show a marked time-saving since the introduction of the MREC. The delays remain at a local level.

The research ethics committee has a dual role. First, it should protect research subjects and patients from exposure to unethical risks or invasions of privacy. Second, it should facilitate ethically acceptable attempts to find new and better treatments from which all may benefit. With these in mind there are three key questions that each researcher and the associated ethics committee should consider:

- is this research important?

- will the research as proposed answer the research question?

- how will the consent of participating patients be obtained, and will this be informed and without coercion?

Many researchers continue to spend large amounts of time in developing arguments about clinical importance and statistical analysis without spending the equivalent amount of time considering issues of patient consent, data privacy and possible coercion. The latter is not usually deliberate but occurs by omission rather than commission.

Areas of ethical tension

There are three main areas of ethical concern at the present time. The first is the use of an evidence-based approach to determine not only clinical practice but also the allocation of scarce resources. The second is the issue of informed consent particularly in patient groups who have impaired autonomy either as a result of age or medical illness. The third is the use of human material removed either as part of normal clinical care or after death.

Evidence-based practice

There is little controversy around the need to use evidence to inform the use of new and existing clinical interventions. The problems arise in the definitions of satisfactory evidence. It is widely accepted that much of NHS research is driven by the biomedical paradigm which itself is dominated by the proof of clinical effectiveness as determined by well-constructed, well-conducted randomised controlled trials (RCTs). The importance of such trials has allowed the development and acceptance by many, of a hierarchy of importance. In this hierarchy the RCT, and subsequent meta-analyses, dominate with case series, cohort studies and professional opinions relegated to relative unimportance. The dominance of the RCT as the gold standard for evidence-based practice has produced three ethical concerns.

First, most RCTs are expensive to run and complicated to organise. There are almost certainly insufficient resources within the NHS R&D funding to support all necessary RCTs. Consequently, most randomised trials are funded by external agencies, particularly the pharmaceutical industry. Their interest is usually directed toward collecting sufficient information about efficacy and safety to satisfy the regulatory authorities prior to the new pharmaceutical preparations being licensed. Therefore, there will be a risk that most RCTs will be conducted on new drugs that are directed toward short-term health problems, and chronic diseases and non-pharmaceutical interventions will not be adequately studied. Second, there may be a temptation for policy makers and health service managers to focus resources on areas for which there is good RCT evidence of clinical effectiveness, for example, new drugs for heart disease. Finally, the absence of RCT evidence of effectiveness does not mean that an intervention is clinically ineffective; it simply means that the necessary studies have not been conducted. Further decisions about resource allocation will utilise RCTs in their proper context, that is, as part of the jigsaw of evidence that will be required to make political decisions.

In establishing or conducting a randomised controlled trial it is implicit that an available therapy of known efficacy is to be compared with a therapy of unknown efficacy. In a randomised, placebo-controlled trial a therapy of uncertain efficacy is compared with an agent of presumed zero efficacy. When it is not clear which therapy is better (new versus old, new versus none, established versus none) there is said to be equipoise on the part of the researcher. Before individual patients can be involved in a RCT, both the individual patient and his or her physician should be assured that there is a true state of equipoise. If neither are assured of this then the trial is unethical.

Informed consent

The current internationally accepted codes for ethical research confirm that participation in clinical research requires that the individual participant should be able to exert their own personal autonomy. Clearly, there are issues to be considered in respect of those who are incompetent, for example, young children and infants and the demented elderly.

It is now clear that age alone is not a useful guide for determining the age of consent. There are many junior school-age children who are quite capable of understanding what the research is about and how it fits in with their lives. This is particularly true for children with chronic health problems, for example, diabetes, chronic arthritis and chronic bowel disease. Consequently, it is now recommended that researchers should enter into partnership arrangements with not only the child but also the family. Only by involving these parties in the process will relevant research-based evidence be collected, which will develop the scientific basis for paediatric practice. Ethics committees need to be reassured that such partnership arrangements are in place for appropriately aged children. For neonates, toddlers and the unconscious child the research needs to have high scientific validity and importance. Strictly speaking, altruistic research (which will have no direct benefit for the involved individual) is not allowed in children. In such a situation ethics committees need to be assured that: the results could not be obtained in any other way; the risk to the child is minimal; and the question being addressed is of a high scientific importance. It is worth reminding the reader that parents are not allowed to volunteer their children for research.

The issues of informed consent outlined above apply equally to the elderly incompetent. In this situation assent, not consent, can be offered by relatives. Assent can be taken as a form of substituted judgement on behalf of the subject. It is unusual for the subject to be so incompetent that they are unable to understand the information that is presented to them, providing of course, the presentation is appropriate.

Currently, the most contentious issue relates to privacy, confidentiality and clinical information sharing. This is particularly true for those who are running, or planning to run, a disease-based register. Both the Data Protection Act of 1998 and the European Bill of Human Rights, incorporated into English and Welsh law in October 2000, confirm that individuals are entitled to privacy and confidentiality in respect of their lives. The current advice to researchers is to ensure that all participants in such registers should give written informed consent for the data to be used for research purposes. This means that the data may be accessed by researchers who may not be the original collector of such data (who is usually the patient's own physician).

The use of human materials

Although this topic has received most publicity and been the source of extensive professional concern in the context of tissues and organs retained after autopsy, there is increasing consideration of the issues associated with the use of surgically removed tissue.

The issue of material retained after autopsy first gained public prominence during the public enquiry into the events surrounding the deaths of children undergoing cardiac surgery in Bristol. It emerged that it was commonplace for entire organs to be retained for the purposes of training, education and research. The salient points to emerge in the subsequent debate were that there was uncertainty about the legality of the retention, and there was widespread public concern about the nature of the consent that had been given for such retention. Suffice it to say that the law is unclear as to who has the right to remove and retain organs from a dead body. If death has been subject to a coroner's enquiry the right is limited to such as is necessary to ascertain the cause of death. If the death has been investigated by an autopsy conducted with permission of the relatives the position is far from clear. What is clear is that relatives did not understand the standard phrase used on autopsy permission forms which referred to the 'removal and retention of tissue' to encompass the retention, without explicit permission, of entire organs. In the living patient informed consent is a requirement before any manoeuvre that would otherwise be considered a battery. Obviously this is a meaningless concept in the case of the dead and since there is no property in a dead body there is legal uncertainty as to what permission should be sought from whom to do what.

The problem that has emerged following the revelations at Bristol (and at many other hospitals) is not whether permission should be sought from relatives (that has long been accepted practice) but exactly how detailed that permission should be. What we are seeing, in effect, is the argument that the principle of informed consent should be applied to the process, even though strictly speaking the concept of consent is not applicable. Relatives expect to be asked to give permission for an autopsy examination and they expect that they will be informed, and given a choice, over what tissues and organs will be retained, and for what purpose(s). These issues are particularly relevant to the case of deaths in children because of the emotional context, and the parallels with the principle of assent (*see* above) are obvious. The preliminary report of the Bristol enquiry, specifically addressed these issues and concluded that whilst professionally sanctioned guidelines might embody best practice they were unenforceable without regulations or legislation. The view was also expressed that even in the context of a coroner's autopsy relatives should be informed if organs have been retained. It appears that the law does not, as yet, embody the views of society. Whilst it would seem clear that any future organ retention, which is explicitly for research, should be done with the knowledge of relatives, it is currently unclear what the position is with archived material removed over many years during the course of autopsy examinations.

The issue of archive material removed in the course of surgical treatment raises similar concerns. Is it ethical to use this tissue for research when it was removed (with consent) as a part of treatment, but without explicit permission for its subsequent use in research? Prospective tissue collection and retention for the purpose of research would be best undertaken with the explicit knowledge and understanding of the patient concerned. Even if the need for consent can be contested the public expectation is that people will be informed of what is to be done. The prudent approach is to obtain separate explicit consent when the removed tissue is intended to be used for research (either already planned, or the creation of a tissue bank for future studies); where the material to be used is in archives then the advice of the chairman of the local Research Ethics Committee should be sought. The implicit consent contained in the process of informed consent for treatment should not be relied upon. In summary, if the use for research can be foreseen the patient should be informed and by implication given the right to withhold permission. In all cases the opinion of an ethics committee should be sought on the potential for harm to patients from the future research as much as from the retention *per se*.

Summary

Despite the introduction of new mechanisms for ethical scrutiny of research there remains inequity of opinion across the NHS. Researchers do not seem to expend sufficient effort in considering the ethical issues that their research may generate. This is particularly true for informed consent and the avoidance of coercion. There remain continuing difficulties in respect of older children, adolescents and the incompetent adult. It appears that many of these problems require the research team to take extra care and effort to ensure that the information necessary to obtain informed consent is presented to subjects in an appropriate way. Only rarely will researchers need to resort to assent from relatives. Consent to the use of removed tissues for research based on custom and practice should no longer be assumed and appropriate advice should be sought from local ethics committees. The research climate is changing with more and more patients wishing to be involved not only in the conduct of research but also in its design. This partnership approach will need to be emphasised in future if patients wish to receive the most effective and appropriate care from the NHS. An understanding of the principles of medical ethics will not necessarily result in easy solutions to complex problems but it may increase the openness of the decision-making process.

Further reading

- Beauchamp TL and Childress JF (1994) *Principles of Biomedical Ethics,* 4th edition. Oxford University Press, Oxford.
  This is a good introduction to modern biomedical ethics. Although US-based it still offers good accessible reading.
- NHS Executive (West Midlands) (2000) *Report of the Review into the Research Framework in North Staffordshire.* NHS Executive (West Midlands).
  This official report considers how, in practice, research should be conducted in children and neonates.
- Hoagwood K, Jensen PS and Fisher CB (1996) *Ethical Issues in Mental Health Research with Children and Adolescents.* Lawrence Erlbaum, Hillsdale, NJ.
  This is a definitive, US-based, series of interlinked papers that consider difficult problems in difficult circumstances.

- Foster CG (1992) The development and future of research ethics committees in Britain. In: A Grubb (ed) *Choices and Decisions in Health Care.* John Wiley, Chichester.
- Jarvis R (1996) Ethical review of medical research and health policy. In: D Greaves and H Upton (eds) *Philosophical Problems in Health Care.* Ashgate, Aldershot.
- National Bioethics Advisory Commission (2000) Research involving human biological materials: ethical issues and policy guidance. *Bull Med Ethics.* **January**:17–22.
  Although aimed at the US research community much of this review is relevant to the UK.
- The Inquiry into the management of care of children receiving complex heart surgery at The Bristol Royal Infirmary (May 2000). *Interim Report – Removal and retention of human material.*
  This report contains an extensive review of the legal and ethical issues relating to the retention and use of human material for research and teaching.
- CPMP Working Party on Efficacy of Medicinal Products (1990) Good clinical practice for trials on medicinal products in the European Community. *Pharmacol Toxicol.* **67**:361–72.
  Although specifically concerned with pharmaceutical trials most of the principles have wider applicability.

8

R&D in primary care: health services research

HUGH GRAVELLE AND DAVID WILKIN

Introduction

The term 'primary healthcare' has many different definitions and even more uses.[1] The World Health Organization applies a broad public health oriented definition encompassing food supply, sanitation, health promotion and disease prevention, as well as the more commonly recognised first contact and continuing healthcare services.[2] In the US and the UK, the term has usually been defined in terms of a service delivery system characterised by generalist clinical care, community-based services, direct access, continuing care and comprehensive coverage (*see* for example references 3, 4). While there is no universally accepted definition, in the UK NHS primary healthcare usually refers to generalist first-contact and continuing care provided by doctors, nurses and a wide range of other health professionals working in the community.

Primary care research encompasses research *by* primary care practitioners, research which takes place *in* primary care and research *on* primary care. The first includes research undertaken *by* GPs, nurses and other healthcare professionals working in primary care settings. The second, research *in* primary care, includes studies where patient recruitment and data collection is mainly carried out in primary care, but the research questions are not specifically primary care related. Examples are drug trials or epidemiological studies. Research *on* primary care relates specifically to the activities of primary care professionals, primary care organisations and patients. Examples are studies of the quality of care, access to services, and patient satisfaction. These broad categories are by no means exclusive so that research by primary care professionals might be focused on primary care provision or might be addressing research questions which are not specifically primary care related. Our focus is research on primary care, whether conducted by primary care professionals or others.

Primary care research has been the subject of two major reviews in recent years by the NHS Executive[5] and the Medical Research Council[4] which provide overviews of research capacity and priorities for future research. Previous editions of this volume have dealt extensively with research by primary care professionals but have paid less attention to health policy and health services research in this area.[6,7] Accordingly, we will concentrate on health services research (HSR).

HSR aims to generate knowledge to improve the health of the community by enhancing the efficiency and effectiveness of the health system. Within the NHS, HSR has tended to be more narrowly defined as '... the identification of the health-care needs of the community and the study of provision, effectiveness and use of the health service'.[8] It aims explicitly to inform health policy, service development and healthcare practice. HSR is not a discipline but an area of applied research where many disciplines, ideas and research methods meet to address common questions. It brings together health professions (medicine, nursing, pharmacy, etc.), epidemiology, statistics, economics, sociology, psychology and other social sciences. It is characterised by alliances between disciplines, theories and methods sharing a common quest to solve problems and generate knowledge. Much HSR is closely linked to initiatives in national, regional and local health policy, not least because most research funding is provided by bodies responsible for the formulation and implementation of health policy. Proximity to policy is both an advantage and a disadvantage. It provides opportunities to undertake research which is directly relevant to decision making. However, closeness to policy means that HSR can be subject to considerable pressures to respond to changes in policy, regardless of whether these are evidence based. Policy makers tend to have rather shorter time horizons than researchers and to want evidence that their policies are working before their effects can properly be assessed.

HSR in primary healthcare focuses on the funding, organisation, delivery and use of services in community settings. It is a wide-ranging area of research involving primary care professions, managers and all of the relevant disciplines. In this chapter we provide a sample of the scope of and opportunities for HSR in primary care. We do so by giving a review of the research agenda for HSR in a key area of NHS policy and service development, the establishment of primary care groups and primary care trusts (PCG/Ts). Even with a focus on PCG/Ts a comprehensive account would take more space than we have available, so the following sections contain a selective view of some of the important areas for research in primary care. It does not even completely reflect the work of our own institution, the National Primary Care Research and Development Centre (NPCRDC), though a fuller account is available from www.nprcdc.ac.uk.

A database of current research on PCG/Ts is being compiled by NPCRDC in collaboration with the Royal College of General Practitioners (RCGP) and will be available via the RCGP website (www.rcgp.org.uk).

NPCRDC is also carrying out two other projects which will provide unique data sets for use by the NHS and by other academic researchers. The first, undertaken with the assistance of the King's Fund, is the Tracker Survey of PCG/Ts[9] which monitors a representative sample of PCG/Ts over time. Data is collected from PCG/T chairs, chief executives, board members, and those with lead responsibilities for key areas such as IM&T and clinical governance. The survey is designed to monitor development of the main PCG/T functions (health improvements, improving primary and community health services and commissioning hospital services). The first round was carried out in Autumn 1999 and published in May 2000 and is being repeated annually. The Tracker Survey provides a unique systematic account of the progress of PCG/Ts in grappling with their new roles. It will inform policy makers and others about the initial and long-term impacts of the new organisational structures.

The second resource being created is the National Database of PCG/Ts which covers all PCG/Ts in England (www.rrl.man.ac.uk/npcgdb). The core database, which is now complete, links information about population socio-economic and demographic characteristics and health status derived from the Office of National Statistics Census to indicators of the organisation and provision of primary care from the annual GP census. It will be a research resource for primary care and a management tool for monitoring and evaluating the performance of PCG/Ts.

The PCG/T research agenda

The establishment of PCGs in April 1999, and their anticipated progression to become PCTs, is the organisational centrepiece of the Labour government's NHS reforms.[10,11] The government fulfilled its manifesto pledge to abolish GP fundholding, but PCGs represent a much more significant change than this. They are expected to play a major role in the local health economy, contributing to improving the health of the population, reducing inequalities, managing the healthcare budget, developing primary care services, commissioning hospital services and working in partnership with other agencies to deliver integrated care. Taken together with the provisions of the NHS (Primary Care) Act of 1997 and the Health Act 1999, the changes to the funding, organisation and provision of primary care are quite revolutionary. For the first time since 1948 the NHS has a single budget for the provision of healthcare for a population. While most GPs remain independent contractors, they are now collectively responsible for delivering high-quality care, better access, improved health and reduced inequalities. As PCGs become PCTs they will take responsibility for providing and managing health services for their populations, employing staff and commissioning hospital services. The 1999 Health Act also allows them to work more closely with social services by pooling budgets and integrating health- and social-care provision. In short, these newly established organisations have the opportunity to become comprehensive managed care organisations, responsible for providing or commissioning all healthcare and key elements of social care for defined populations.

The advent of PCG/Ts will change the context in which all primary care research is carried out, whether epidemiological research, treatment trials or health system evaluation. However, for health services research in primary care such major policy initiatives also require a reappraisal of the research agenda. This is not to imply that research should follow each twist and turn of policy. It should address underlying and robust research questions, the answers to which will be useful whatever the current policy. However, the advent of major changes inevitably requires some reformulation of the questions to ensure that the results of the research meet their aim of informing policy and supporting implementation. In the following sections we outline some of the important research questions for primary care HSR to inform the development of PCGs and PCTs.

Organisation of PCG/Ts

PCG/Ts are a new form of organisation in a service where there is little previous experience of collective governance, accountability or wider stakeholder participation. The NHS has long experience of hierarchical organisations (e.g. hospitals and health authorities) and more recent experience during the 1990s of using market mechanisms. The former have proved rigid and difficult to change, while the latter proved unpopular and failed to fully deliver the hoped-for gains in effectiveness and efficiency.[12] Neither is likely to prove a wholly satisfactory model for managing a complex network of independent contractors, employees and commissioned services. PCGs and PCTs are an experiment in developing alternative approaches to governance, founded on the participation and engagement of local stakeholders. Within a broadly prescribed framework of Board membership and officers, there is considerable scope for local variation. PCTs will vary in size, services provided and governance arrangements, possibly leading to a variety of organisational models which may be adapted to local circumstances. Research has an important role to play in helping to define the needs of these new organisations, evaluating their capacity to deliver change, identifying features associated with success and highlighting obstacles and barriers.

Structure and governance

PCG/Ts vary in size (from around 50 000 to more than 200 000 population), management capacity and roles, degree of centralisation and decision-making mechanisms. They will be able to employ a mix of regulation, contracts, incentives and education to influence service development and to change professional behaviour. Research is needed to examine the effects of different structures and governance arrangements on the quality and quantity of services provided. There is also some evidence from other parts of the NHS[13,14] that size of organisations affects their performance, but there has been no work based on experience in PCG/Ts.

Accountability

The creation of new organisations with very substantial responsibilities raises questions about how to manage their performance and how to hold them accountable. PCG/Ts are accountable through annual accountability agreements to health authorities (HAs) who retain overall responsibility for strategic direction. Research is needed to inform the development of appropriate performance indicators for PCG/Ts and to assess the effectiveness of mechanisms for holding them to account. On the other side, PCG/Ts will have to develop performance criteria and accountability mechanisms for the organisations and individuals providing services, including GPs, community services and hospital services. Research is needed to develop and evaluate performance indicators and accountability mechanisms between the PCG/Ts and those who provide services.

Information

Effective and efficient strategic planning and management of the services for which PCG/Ts are responsible will only be achieved if they have access to appropriate, reliable and timely information. While much of the necessary data is already collected within the NHS, PCG/Ts will have to have systems which enable them to access and use it. In particular, they will need to develop links with general practices, community and hospital providers. Research in this area can help to clarify their information needs and assess the effectiveness of alternative approaches to accessing data.

Engaging stakeholders

Local involvement and responsiveness to local needs were a major part of the rationale for the establishment of PCGs. PCG/Ts are intended to place GPs, nurses, social services and the local community at the forefront of the development of health services. To achieve this requires processes and mechanisms which facilitate communication and participation by professionals and local communities. While the composition of Boards and Executive Committees guarantees representation of key stakeholders, it does not engage stakeholders outside the organisation. Research is needed to evaluate strategies for communicating with and involving professional and lay stakeholders in decision making.

Resources

Budgets

The way in which the financial structure of the NHS influences its performance is determined by the answers to four questions (*see* Box 8.1). The introduction of PCG/Ts was associated with changes in the answers to the first three. Hospital and community health service (HCHS) budgets have been allocated to HAs by national formulae increasingly based on weighted capitation. Weighted capitation is also now used to determine the allocations for prescribing and general medical service cash limited (GMS-CL) expenditure on practice infrastructure, staff and computing. The resulting total budget for the HA is then allocated by them to PCG/Ts, though HAs need not apply the national formulae to determine the total budget for their PCG/Ts.

Box 8.1: Crucial questions concerning budgets

	Pre PCG/T era	PCG/T era
How are budgets determined?	Weighted capitation for HCHS; history for prescribing, GMS-CL. No budget for GMS	Weighted capitation No budget for GMS
What may they be spent on?	Separate budgets for HCHS, prescribing, GMS-CL	Unified budget
Who holds the budget?	HAs; fundholding practices	PCG/Ts
Who takes expenditure decisions?	GPs	GPs

There are strong *prima facie* arguments for replacing allocation by decibel or historical accident by formulae based on explicit measures of need, for removing artificial boundaries between budget headings which prevent the use of resources where they are most effective in pursuing PCG/T objectives and for moving budgetary responsibility closer to the GPs who actually make the prescribing and referral decisions which determine PCG/T expenditure.

However, significant issues remain. The national formulae are necessarily crude because of data limitations. The lower the level at which formulae are applied to determine budgets the more detailed and sensitive they have to be to ensure that needs are properly captured since variations in need become more pronounced the smaller the population. The White Paper *The New NHS: modern, dependable* envisaged that budgets would eventually be extended from PCG/Ts to practices and linked to financial incentives. PCG/Ts were required to put prescribing incentive schemes in place in 1999–2000 and many were linked to prescribing budgets. Thus PCG/Ts will want to develop their own formulae based on local data as they attempt to allocate budgets to practice level in line with the White Paper suggestion. They will have to carry out their own need assessments which will require research on their local populations.

Even when practice population needs can be measured in the sense that effect of population characteristics on expected need for care is known, there is a second problem: actual realised need in any year may differ substantially from expected need. Practice populations are likely to be too small for random fluctuations at the level of individual patients to cancel out on average.[15] But if budgets are not held at individual practice level incentives to take proper account of the costs of referral and prescribing are seriously attenuated. Hence, there is scope for research on alternative methods of managing risks, from holding budgets at different levels to risk sharing and insurance arrangements.[16]

Incentives

The creation of PCG/Ts has been associated with changes in the explicit and implicit incentive system for GPs. PCG/Ts are required to have prescribing incentive schemes and there is pressure on them to extend practice budgets to HCHS and to link them to incentives. HAs and PCTs are able to negotiate contracts with practices, including salaried status, for the supply of personal medical services (PMS), without being constrained by the standard 'Red Book'. The National Plan envisages that a substantial minority of GPs will be on such contracts by 2004.[11] There is considerable evidence that GPs respond to incentives[17-19] but little information on the effects of the particular arrangements in PCG/Ts. There is some preliminary evidence about the forms of PMS contracts[20] but as yet there is no evaluation of their effect on the behaviour of GPs.

Cost-effective use of resources

The cost effectiveness of much (most?) of primary care activity has still to be evaluated. PCG/Ts and practices will need to consider:

- what activities are worthwhile?

- how should they be carried out?

- where: in primary care, specialist outreach clinics, or secondary care settings?[21-22]

- who by: should nurses or GPs provide certain types of service?[23]

- what is the appropriate role for self-care by patients?

Quality and clinical governance

PCG/Ts now have responsibility for clinical governance of their practices to encourage good quality. At the least this will require PCG/Ts to ensure that their practices follow guidelines such as those being developed by the National Institute for Clinical Excellence. Many will want to play a more active role in reducing variations in the quality of care across practices and in increasing the average quality of care received. This will require the ability to measure the quality of care, to recognise unacceptable variations in quality and to provide the information and motivation for primary care teams to improve the quality of their care.

Measuring quality

There are relatively few indicators of quality in primary care which are both evidence-based and available without disproportionate effort.[24] There is no means of routinely measuring patient satisfaction and experience in practices. Special surveys will be required. Some instruments, such as the General Practitioner Assessment Survey and the Patient Enablement Instrument[25] have been developed but may not cover all aspects of practices which patients believe to be important. Very little is known about patients' relative valuations of practice attributes. Without such information it is not possible to use measures of patients' views to inform many aspects of decisions about practice quality; for example, would patients prefer to have longer consultations or to have more consultations with a shorter waiting time? There have been some attempts to apply methods such as conjoint analysis[26] to these types of question but much remains to be done.

Variations in quality: comparing like with like

Practices use a mix of inputs to produce a large set of outputs. In evaluating performance on one dimension, account must be taken of performance on all the other dimensions. We need to allow for the other outputs and their quality as well as the inputs used in order to properly compare 'like with like'. 'Confounding' is a fundamental problem whenever a single indicator is used to reflect a single dimension of performance.[27] A practice may score badly on a particular indicator, such as the proportion of high-risk patients receiving influenza vaccinations, because it is inefficient or because:

- it is using its resources to produce higher quality in other respects (better health promotion, or child surveillance, or better quality consultations)

- it is producing more of other types of services (more minor surgery, more night visits)

- it is using fewer resources

- it is operating in a less favourable socio-economic environment than other practices

- the indicator is adversely affected by variables controlled in other sectors over which it has no influence.

Indicators can alert PCG/Ts to the possibility of unusually good or poor performance but, to ensure that like is truly compared with like, PCG/Ts will need to undertake systematic research with techniques such as multiple regression modelling to allow for the way in which performance indicators can be confounded in their local conditions.[28]

Motivating good practice

PCG/Ts may help practices to improve quality by providing information to them, but they may also want to consider more direct methods.[29] One possibility is public disclosure of information on practice performance. The evidence to date on the effects of public disclosure of quality information is quite limited, and relates mainly to US secondary care.[30] There is therefore opportunity for controlled experimentation in the UK primary care context to examine the effects of disclosure.

It is also possible to link performance measures to incentives, as with many prescribing incentive schemes. Some PCG/Ts have provided financial rewards to practices for keeping referral rates for some conditions within certain bands. Research is required to evaluate different incentive schemes to investigate whether their designers have succeeded in avoiding the dysfunctional consequences suggested by some commentators,[31] whether financial rewards are preferable to non-financial, whether financial rewards should take the form of an increase in funds to be spent for the benefit of practice patients or whether they should be given as additional practice income, and whether team or individual rewards are more effective.

Population health and primary care

PCG/Ts are required to take a population focus in their policies, in particular to encourage improvement in the health of their populations and to reduce the extent of inequity. In order to do so they must address a number of crucial issues, each of which currently has a small evidence base.

The first issue is whether the primary care services make any difference to population health. The arguments of McKeown[32] that healthcare has little effect on population health have been questioned on the basis of more recent investigations which suggest that modern healthcare can make a difference.[33] However, there have been few studies of the relationship between primary care provision and health outcomes[34] and those have been at high levels of aggregation. Little is known about the way in which differences in primary care resources and delivery can affect population health.

Unless utilisation of primary care by the population is amenable to policy decisions that change the level of resources or the way in which they are delivered, the fact that primary care can affect health may have little relevance for policy. Thus, the second issue is how the use of primary care is determined by the characteristics of the populations served[35] and the way in which the service is delivered.

Finally, PCG/Ts need to know the extent of avoidable inequity in primary care. There are both methodological[36] and empirical questions to be resolved. What aspect of inequity matters: is the focus on access, use, amount of resources consumed, health, or health gain? What factors should *not* affect these dimensions: income, education, age, gender …? How should inequity at individual level be aggregated to give a summary measure so that progress at PCG/T or practice level can be monitored? Does the extent of inequity vary with factors, such as practice organisation and policies or resourcing which can be influenced by PCG/T initiatives?

Conclusion

We built our discussion of the health services research needs in primary care around the issues which PCG/Ts will face. There is great diversity of PCG/Ts in terms of their size, their structure, the emphasis they place on different objectives, the resources available and the populations for whom they must deliver and commission services. Such diversity is both a problem and an opportunity for health services research. It is a problem because it may reduce the applicability of results based on studies on small numbers of PCG/Ts and researchers need to take account of the issue when designing their research strategies. It is an opportunity for health service researchers and policy makers because it provides a much richer set of data on alternative possible solutions to policy problems. Health services research can play a crucial role in documenting and evaluating alternative solutions and in helping to disseminate the 'best practice' so discovered.

Acknowledgement

Funding from the Department of Health to the NPCRDC is acknowledged. The views expressed by the authors are not necessarily those of the Department of Health.

References

1 Pedersen LL and Wilkin D (1998) Primary health care: definitions, users and uses, *Health Care Anal.* **6**:341–51.
2 WHO (1978) *Primary Health Care.* Report of the International Conference on Primary Health Care, Alma-Ata, USSR,

6–12 September [*Health for All Series*, No. 1]. World Health Organization, Geneva.

3   Starfield B (1993) Primary care. *J Ambulat Care Manag.* **16**(4):27–37.

4   Medical Research Council (1997) *MRC Topic Review: primary health care.* Medical Research Council, London.

5   Mant D (1997) *R&D in Primary Care.* Report of the National Working Group, November. NHSE, London.

6   Heywood P (1998) Research and development in primary care. In: M Baker and S Kirk (eds) *Research and Development for the NHS: evidence, evaluation and effectiveness* (2e). Radcliffe Medical Press, Oxford.

7   Evans A (1996) Research in primary care settings and at the interface with secondary care. In: M Baker and S Kirk (eds) *Research and Development for the NHS: evidence, evaluation and effectiveness* (1e). Radcliffe Medical Press, Oxford.

8   Clarke M and Kurinczak JJ (1992) Health services research: a case of need or special pleading? The Committee of Heads of Academic Departments of Public Health. *BMJ.* **304**:165–6.

9   Wilkin D, Gillam S and Leese B (eds) (2000) *National Tracker Survey of Primary Care Groups and Trusts: progress and challenges 1999/2000.* NPCRDC, University of Manchester.

10 Department of Health (1997) *The New NHS: modern, dependable.* HMSO, London.

11 Department of Health (2000) *The NHS Plan,* Cm 4818-I, July. HMSO, London.

12 Le Grand J, Mays N and Mulligan J (eds) (1998) *Learning from the NHS Internal Market.* King's Fund, London.

13 Ferguson B, Posnett J and Sheldon T (eds) (1997) *Concentration and Choice in Healthcare.* Royal Society of Medicine Press, Edinburgh.

14 Giuffrida A, Gravelle H and Sutton M (2000) Efficiency and administrative costs in primary care. *J Health Econ.* **19**(6):983–1006.

15 Martin S, Rice N and Smith PC (1997) Risk and the GP Budgetholder, Discussion Paper No. 153. Centre for Health Economics, University of York.

16 Baxter K, Bachman M and Bevan G (2000) Primary care groups: trade-offs in managing budgets and risk. *Public Money and Management*. **January–March**:53–62.

17 Gosden T, Forland F, Kristiansen IS *et al.* (2000) Capitation, salaried, fee for service and mixed systems of payment: effects on the behaviour of Primary Care Physicians [Review]. In: L Bero, R Grilli, J Grimshaw and A Oxman (eds) Collaboration on Effective Professional Practice Module of The Cochrane Database of Systematic Reviews. The Cochrane Library Update Software, Oxford.

18 Giuffrida A, Leese B, Forland F *et al.* (2000) Target payments in primary care: effects on professional practice and health outcomes [Review]. In: L Bero, R Grilli, J Grimshaw and A Oxman (eds) Collaboration on Effective Professional Practice Module of The Cochrane Database of Systematic Reviews. The Cochrane Library Update Software, Oxford.

19 Croxson B, Propper C and Perkins A (2001) Do doctors respond to financial incentives? UK family doctors and the GP fundholding scheme. *J Public Econ.* **79**(2): 375–98.

20 Sheaff R and Lloyd-Kendall A (2000) Principal-agent relationships in general practice: the first wave of English Personal Medical Services pilot contracts. *J Health Serv Res Policy.* **5**(3):156–63.

21 Godber E, Robinson R and Steiner A (1997) Economic evaluation and the shifting balance towards primary care: definitions, evidence and methodological issues. *Health Econ.* **6**:275–94.

22 Pedersen LL and Leese B (1997) What will a primary care led NHS mean for GP workload? The problem of the lack of evidence base. *BMJ.* **314**:1337–41.

23 Halliwell S, Sibbald B and Rose S (1999) *A Bibliography of Skill Mix in Primary Care – The Sequel.* National Primary Research and Development Centre, Manchester.

24 Campbell SM, Roland MO, Quayle JA *et al.* (1998) Quality indicators for general practice: which ones can general practitioners and health authority managers agree are important and how useful are they? *J Public Health Med.* **20**:414–21.

25 Howie JGR, Heaney DJ and Maxwell MA (1998) A comparison of the Patient Enablement Instrument (PEI) against two established satisfaction scales as an outcome measure of primary care consultations. *Fam Pract.* **15**: 165–71.

26 Scott A and Vick S (1999) Patients, doctors and contracts: an application of principal-agent theory to the doctor-patient relationship. *Scot J Pol Econ.* **46**:111–32.

27 Giuffrida A, Gravelle H and Roland M (1999) Measuring quality of care with routine data: performance indicators should not be confused with health outcomes. *BMJ.* **319**:94–8.

28 Gravelle H, Dusheiko M and Sutton M (2000) Rationing by time and money in the NHS: variations in admission rates. Centre for Health Economics Technical Paper No. TP17. Centre for Health Economics, University of York.

29 NHS Centre for Reviews and Dissemination (1999) Getting evidence into practice. *Effective Health Care Bull.* **5**(1):February.

30 Marshall M, Shekell PG, Leatherman S and Brook RH (2000) The public release of performance data: what do we expect to gain? A review of the evidence. *JAMA.* **283**(14):1866–74.

31 Smith PC (1995) On the unintended consequences of publishing performance data in the public sector. *Int J Public Admin.* **18**:277–310.

32 McKeown T (1979) *The Role of Medicine: dream, mirage or nemesis?* Blackwell, Oxford.

33 Mackenbach J (1996) The contribution of medical care to mortality decline: Mckeown revisited. *J Clin Epidemiol.* **49**:1207–13.

34 Baker D and Klein R (1991) Explaining outputs of primary care: population and practice factors. *BMJ.* **303**:225–9.

35 Campbell SM and Roland MO (1996) Why do people consult the doctor? *Fam Pract.* **13**:75–83.

36 Culyer AJ and Wagstaff A (1992) Equity and equality in health and health care. *J Health Econ.* **12**:431–57.

9

Health services research

BRIAN FERGUSON, ANTONY FRANKS AND
STEPHEN HARRISON

Introduction

Like all other forms of research, the objective of health service research (HSR) is to obtain new knowledge. Unlike some other forms of research, HSR is aimed at producing knowledge which is of more-or-less immediate application as a means of reducing the uncertainties of what healthcare is worth providing, to whom, and how to organise it. The hierarchy of evidence[1] according to which the results of randomised controlled trials (RCTs), aggregated through meta-analysis and other forms of systematic review, constitute the highest level or 'gold standard' has come to be seen as providing the defining scale of validity for such research. In the first section of this chapter we outline the main elements of, and rationales for such designs. Decisions about whether to provide particular healthcare interventions may well, however, hinge on more than the question of 'what works'. Health technologies can rarely be allocated to simple categories of 'effective' or 'ineffective'. Rather, they can be located on a spectrum of probabilities of effectiveness; what is the chance that intervention X will work for this class of patient? Moreover, resources are finite and different technologies have different financial and opportunity costs, so that a rational consideration of the effectiveness of a health technology would include some kind of calculus aimed at incorporating such factors. Such a calculus is conventionally provided by some of the techniques of microeconomic analysis, and the second section of this chapter offers a brief account of these before discussing some broader questions of economic appraisal in healthcare. The final section addresses the methodological consequences of researching 'diffuse' technologies, that is those where the intervention is multifaceted, difficult to specify, and/or depends extensively on *social* causes and effects.

Randomised controlled trials

Any evaluation of a therapy involves a comparison; either with an inactive agent – a placebo (to ask whether the intervention has any effect, beneficial or otherwise) – or, more commonly, with an established therapy (to ask whether it offers any benefit over the current alternatives). In making such comparisons it is possible to select patients for each group in such a way that any desired result is more likely. Thus if the desire is to demonstrate benefit from a new agent then patients judged to be likely to respond well (perhaps because they have a milder or self-limiting form of the disease in question) could be selected for the group in whom the new agent is administered, while those judged unlikely to respond could be allocated to the placebo group. This is *selection bias*. Whilst rarely as blatant as described above, the possibility that it might operate at a subconscious level requires some method of selection that will minimise any suspicion that there has been bias in the construction of the two groups whose responses to the treatments under study are to be measured. The nature of medical technology development over the past 20 years has been such that newer methods of treatment often offer relatively small proportionate gains over existing alternatives. Whereas a massive difference in benefit of a therapy, say 95% survival with treatment compared to 5% without, would be difficult to achieve without gross selection bias, smaller benefits may be more difficult to detect if the bias operates to cancel out any such effect. Other forms of bias can occur; as a general rule, *biases in measurement and interpretation of outcomes* are minimised by concealing from investigators the allocation (to the treatment or comparison group) of each individual. This is known as 'blinding'. In a single-blind trial the concealment is from either the investigator or the patient; in a double-blind trial neither investigators nor patients know the allocation. Only when the analysis of data is undertaken will the allocation of each individual be known.

Why randomisation?

The allocation of patients to groups by random selection is the key feature of a randomised trial and the key feature of randomisation is that it is not influenced by those undertaking the trial. Prior to the use of randomisation, a number of methods had been used to allocate participants to groups including alternation (by day of entry or simply sequentially) or quasi-random methods such as allocation based on birth date. The first use of randomisation in a clinical trial was in order to separate the decision by physicians to enter patients into the trial from any knowledge of whether the latter would receive streptomycin or an inactive placebo, which in the case of tuberculosis could be a life or death decision.[2] Not only is it desirable to remove, as far as possible, the influence of bias in the selection of participants in each group, but it is also desirable that the two groups are as similar as possible in terms of characteristics that may affect their response to the interventions being compared; these might include stage of disease, age, social class, associated clinical conditions and smoking status. Randomisation *per se* does not guarantee that the resultant groups are the same in all aspects; it simply ensures that any differences have occurred by chance. Whilst it is true that in large studies differences will tend to 'even out', this cannot be assumed. It is therefore essential that, as part of the analysis of the data collected during a trial, attention is paid to the eventual make-up of the groups being compared. If they differ in ways which might affect the outcomes of interest this has to be taken into account in assessing the meaning of the final results. There is a way around these randomly occurring differences but its implementation adds to the complexity of the trial administration. The approach, known as minimisation,[3] actively seeks to construct the groups resulting from random allocation so that they do not differ in the distribution of factors known, or believed, to affect the outcomes under study. Groups may be constructed purely on the basis of the factors possessed by each new entrant, allocation being made in such a way as will minimise the differences between the groups, or be combined with chance. The crucial feature of this type of active allocation is that the allocations of *individual* trial participants are not influenced by those undertaking the study. It is therefore free from selection bias even though the selection is not necessarily random.

Does size matter?

RCTs are expensive to set up and run, and the larger the trial the greater the cost. In committing to such expenditure it is sensible to ensure that the trial proposed will be capable of answering the question(s) posed. There is a mathematically complex, but conceptually simple, relationship between the size of a trial (that is the number of participants in each group) and its ability to answer the questions posed by the researchers. This relationship is embodied in the term 'power'. The power of a trial is its ability to detect a previously defined level of difference between the two groups being studied; it is conventionally presented as (1 – the risk that the trial will miss such a difference) and a value between 80 and 90% is usually sought. The risk that a trial will miss the predefined difference is a measure of the risk of obtaining a false negative; that is that there was a difference but the trial failed to detect it. Overall, the smaller the predefined difference, the larger the trial will have to be to be sure that it will detect such a difference (if it exists) or exclude it (if it does not). Many trials have failed to deliver a conclusive result because they were too small.

Selection of the study population

The population in whom the study is to be conducted should be sufficiently similar to the broad population to whom it is hoped to generalise the findings. It also should be capable of yielding enough individuals for the study to have enough power (*see* above) and be one in which the outcomes to be compared occur with sufficient frequency for the study to be practicable in a defined period of time. The longer a study has to run, the higher its costs; the time it takes to complete a study will be influenced by how quickly participants are recruited to it, the frequency of the outcome studied, and the length of follow-up necessary to ensure a reasonable chance of detecting that outcome. Where the outcome is likely to be measured within the period of a hospital inpatient episode (such as speed of wound healing or frequency of infection) follow-up times will be shorter than if a prolonged period of observation is needed (such as the need for cardiac by-pass surgery in a 5-year period). If the outcome event is a rare one it may be necessary to collect data from more than one centre which obviously increases the complexity and costs of a study, and makes the use of a clear protocol important to ensure that data from each of the centres are comparable in quality and validity.

Principles of analysis

In planning a RCT thought has to be given to the potential value or use of the findings. Two broad categories of study are recognised: the explanatory trial and the pragmatic trial.[4] The explanatory trial is concerned with the underlying cause and effect relationship between an intervention and an outcome; the approach is closer to a laboratory experiment in its philosophy, with carefully selected and probably highly motivated patients. It will have high internal validity; what it appears to demonstrate about the relationship between intervention and an outcome will be more likely to be true. However, its prediction of what will happen when the intervention is transferred to a real-world clinical setting may be poor. A pragmatic trial recognises that, in a clinical setting, patients do not always adhere to treatment protocols and that other events may intervene to prevent completion of a course of treatment. In this case, the trial setting will more closely resemble that of ordinary practice than the laboratory. Its internal validity may be lower but if an effect is shown then it is more likely that this effect will be seen when the intervention is used in settings other than a clinical trial. In both cases equal attention is given to the rigorous selection of participants, the collection of valid data and the maintenance of blinding if required. One manifestation of a pragmatic approach to most modern randomised trials is the use of 'intention-to-treat' analysis. This is based on the recognition that, in real life, adherence to treatment regimes is unlikely to be complete. Any analysis that attempts to 'correct' for non-adherence to the treatments originally allocated, or for patients whose treatment is for whatever reason changed (say from that indicated in one group to that indicated in the comparison group) may produce a result that says, in effect, 'If everyone were to do exactly what they were supposed to then this is the effect you would expect to get'. Whilst this may be useful in understanding a biological relationship between intervention and outcome, it offers little of value to the question 'Is it worth trying in the setting in which I practise?' The key issue for pragmatic trials is the transferability of the finding to the non-research setting. By undertaking intention-to-treat analysis the possibility of missing a true effect is increased but the chance of falsely concluding that a treatment will work in a non-research setting is diminished. On balance the preference is to reduce the risk of a false positive at the expense of increasing the chance of a false negative.

The presentation of results

Data on the outcomes studied (such as death, blood pressure, length of time before a cancer recurs) will be collected from the two comparison groups. The nature of such data and the timescale will depend on the nature of the intervention and the outcomes. The frequency of the outcome of interest (if it is a definable event such as death, a heart attack or a stroke) or its value (if it is a continuous variable such as blood pressure, or a time) is calculated for each group and compared. Where events are measured, the usual summaries of difference are based on the frequencies (or risks) of the event in one group compared to the other. If the comparison is calculated by subtraction, the measure is known as the absolute risk difference (or reduction). If the comparison is calculated by division the measure is known as the relative risk.

Table 9.1: Data for two hypothetical groups in a RCT

	Group A Standard treatment (control group)	Group B Experimental treatment
Outcome of interest at end of trial period	90	35
Total in group	250	250
Risk of event	36%	14%

Table 9.1 sets out data for two hypothetical groups, one on standard treatment, and one on the 'experimental' treatment. We can see that:

• the absolute risk reduction for the experimental treatment is the difference between the risk in Group A and the risk in Group B: 36% – 14%, i.e. 22%, and

• the relative risk for the experimental treatment is the risk in Group B as a proportion of the risk in Group A: 14% ÷ 36% i.e. 0.39.

Because the relative risk is less than 1 this indicates that the outcome is less likely to occur in the experimental treatment; if this outcome is undesirable then the experimental treatment is more effective than the control treatment. In these circumstances a relative risk greater than 1 would indicate that the experimental treatment was less effective than the control treatment.

Experience has shown that people are more impressed by the relative risk even if the absolute benefit from a new treatment is small.[5] As a counter to this, a measure has been developed which provides a broader perspective on the effectiveness of a new treatment. This is the 'number needed to treat' (NNT).[6] It is based on the concept that, given the evidence of effectiveness from a trial, in order to achieve one more benefit (or one undesirable outcome less) than would have been achieved with the standard (or control) treatment a certain number of patients would have to be treated. NNT is simply derived by taking the reciprocal of the absolute risk reduction and multiplying by 100. The data in Table 9.1 would yield an NNT of just over 4.57 ($1 \div 22 \times 100$). This is normally rounded up to the nearest whole number, in this case 5. Where the outcome measures are not analysable as dichotomous variables, they may be presented as survival curves (survival over time) or different summary values in the two groups (such as mean blood pressure, median length of stay) with appropriate statistical analysis to assess any differences.

Meta-analysis

As indicated above, trials may be too small to detect a difference (even if it existed) between two treatments. If the trials have been properly conducted it is possible to combine their data thus, in effect, creating a single trial of adequate size to answer the question. This is the technique of meta-analysis.[7] A meta-analysis may be undertaken with summary data from published studies (meta-analysis from the literature) or with individual patient data obtained from the organisers of the original studies (meta-analysis of individual patient data). This technique requires as complete an ascertainment as possible of all trials (published or not) which meet relevant quality criteria (such as randomisation, blinding, intention-to-treat analysis), and then the use of appropriate methods to combine the data and derive estimates of effect. One serious criticism of this approach is that the combination of data from trials conducted in different populations and possibly with different treatment regimes may not be valid. In addition, the failure to detect trials, particularly those with a negative result, may bias the overall estimate of effect of a treatment.[8]

Economic appraisal

In healthcare, as in any other sector of the economy, resources are scarce in relation to the many competing needs and demands and hence choices have to be made. Economics is fundamentally concerned with the basis for such choice, and holds that decisions should take into account the value of the next-best alternative use of the same resources, a concept labelled 'opportunity cost' by economists. Equally fundamental is the notion that the *marginal* effects of decisions are often the appropriate focus of analysis: do the *additional* benefits of a particular course of action outweigh the *additional* costs? Although such concepts appear intuitively reasonable, they are not followed instinctively by decision makers who will frequently be constrained by past actions ('sunk costs') and focus on the 'average' rather than the marginal effects of policy changes. This is not to say that the economist's view is the 'correct' one, but it is an alternative way of analysing decisions that can frequently highlight new options or cast a different light on existing options for change. Like medicine, economics is not an exact science; it is a social science because at its heart it entails studying human behaviour, which can be both unpredictable and 'irrational'. The analogies with evidence-based medicine (EBM) are illuminating: both economics and medicine have a scientific basis, but the application of EBM has to recognise the limits of the approach, which if taken too far can place a disproportionate emphasis upon guidelines, protocols and a rational, mechanistic approach.[9] Similarly, economics must recognise uncertainty and the fact that people's characteristics and behaviour are unpredictable, varied and complex. In the same way that a clinical guideline cannot possibly legislate for the character-istics of every conceivable individual presenting to the health-care system, the findings of even the best-designed economic appraisal can do no more than *inform* the decision-making process.

The scope of health economic analysis

Economics as a discipline is wider than micro-economic evaluation; the reason for labouring this is that in some circles health economics has become synonymous with economic evaluation, which understates the contribution that economics can make to health and healthcare. Examples of the broad areas where economics could contribute are as follows:

- comparing the cost effectiveness of different drugs
- comparing alternative ways of delivering a rehabilitation service
- prioritising whether to invest more in primary and second-ary prevention of ischaemic heart disease or commissioning more revascularisation procedures
- appraising the cost and benefits of different strategies to reduce the number of childhood accidents
- assessing how much additional investment to make in cancer care compared to mental health services
- appraising the consequences of hospital mergers in terms of cost and quality of care or
- assessing which socio-economic variables to include in resource allocation formulae.

Some of these questions are considered further below, but first it is important to outline briefly the different forms of economic evaluation. For an up-to-date text and full description of these, the reader is referred to Drummond *et al.*[10]

Forms of economic evaluation

There are four techniques that are typically described within economic evaluation: cost-minimisation analysis; cost-effectiveness analysis; cost-benefit analysis and cost-utility analysis.

- *Cost-minimisation analysis* (CMA) is relevant where it is known that the clinical effectiveness of alternative treatments is the same, and the problem reduces to one of finding the least-cost alternative. CMA is really a special case of cost-effectiveness analysis in which the outcomes are known in advance to be equivalent.

- *Cost-effectiveness analysis* (CEA) is relevant where costs can be compared to a single, common treatment effect which may differ in magnitude between alternatives (e.g. cost per life year gained).

- *Cost–benefit analysis* (CBA) is relevant where outcomes cannot be reduced to a single, common effect, and hence a common 'currency' is needed to compare costs and benefits. An obvious example is to use '£' to value costs and benefits and derive cost–benefit ratios associated with the alternatives being compared. Clearly, the monetary valuation of benefits is particularly problematic in evaluating the health and wider consequences of interventions.

- *Cost–utility analysis* (CUA) is preferred by those who have reservations about valuing benefits in monetary terms. In CUA the measure of value is the 'utility' provided by each alternative, where utility is viewed in the widest possible sense to 'refer to the preferences individuals or society may have for any particular set of health outcomes'.[10] A well-known example of a cost-utility measure is the cost per quality-adjusted life year (QALY).[11] This allows outcomes to be expressed in a single index (the QALY) that combines aspects of quality of life and life expectancy. There are, however, alternative generic outcome measures such as healthy years equivalent (HYE).[12]

The whole issue of outcome and utility measurement, as well as the advantages and disadvantages of different measures, remains the subject of much discussion within the health economics community. Whichever form of economic evaluation is adopted, there is a common objective; the analyst is attempting to express the costs and consequences (benefits/ outcomes/effectiveness) in terms which facilitate comparisons between alternative courses of action. In many economic evaluations the comparison is very tightly defined within the context of an RCT (e.g. the costs and effectiveness of drug X versus drug Y), whereas in many other situations decision makers are faced with a more complex, less controlled environment in which to make multifactorial decisions with highly imperfect information. The discipline of economic evaluation becomes arguably even more important in such circumstances.

Wider policy appraisal and health

Not all decisions about health and healthcare provision are neatly-defined choices about medical treatments. This is reflected in the current government's emphasis upon the wider determinants of health (*see*, for example, reference 13) and explicit recognition that healthcare and other sectors have complementary roles to play in improving the health of the population. Thus Health Improvement Programmes (HImPs) and Health Action Zones (HAZs) are aimed both at improving the health of local communities and at reducing unjustified (however defined) inequalities in health. Although any of the above forms of economic evaluation may be relevant, it will almost certainly be the case that the outcomes of wider policies are multidimensional, hence CBA and/or CUA will be appropriate. A hypothetical example would be the appraisal of different strategies aimed at reducing the number of childhood accidents. Some of the costs and consequences of a successful strategy in this area would be:

- a lower burden on hospital A&E services

- greater costs to families in making homes safer

- a reduction in life years lost

- 'externality' effects on family and friends

- reduced 'lost future output' in the economy

- increased cost of road safety

- less pressure on other emergency services.

This list illustrates the complexity of economic appraisal in areas where the outcomes of policy alternatives are multidimensional and cannot easily be reduced to a common denominator. Although the measurement and valuation of outcomes is clearly problematic, the issue of identifying and measuring costs is not straightforward either. It can be seen from the above list that it is important to be clear about the perspective taken in an economic evaluation, so that a decision can be taken about which costs to include or exclude. Costs can fall on private individuals, primary care, hospitals, commissioners of healthcare services, other public sector organisations, and society at large. Economists usually argue that the societal perspective is appropriate, but economic evaluations rarely manage to take into account the full range of costs (or indeed benefits) that would be implied by this purist stance. What is particularly important is that the analysis makes explicit the perspective taken; in many cases a narrower perspective (e.g. costs to the NHS, costs to carers) may be entirely appropriate. (Two useful documents in this area are references 14 and 15.)

Service delivery and organisation

It follows from the above that it is not only the outcome of HTA (narrowly defined) that will provide new knowledge relevant to questions about what healthcare is worth providing and how. There is a permeable boundary between HTA and what has come to be labelled as service delivery and organisation (SDO). Given the almost constant re-configuration of services and structural change that characterises the NHS, industrial economics has much to add in this area. An obvious area for exploration is that of hospital mergers, which although largely politically driven, could be the subject of systematic appraisal in terms of the likely costs and benefits. For example, Goddard and Ferguson[16] concluded from an examination of the literature that there should be no automatic presumption that hospital Trust mergers reduce costs, particularly where not accompanied by a reduction in the number of hospital sites. This conclusion is highly relevant to discussions about 'service alliances' resulting from greater sub-specialisation in clinical care and potential mergers of primary care groups and health authorities. What impact are such alliances and mergers likely to have upon the costs of healthcare, and what benefits to patients will be gained in terms of the quality of care and final outcomes?

Much of the structural change proposed in the NHS rests upon the assumption that greater centralisation of services and/or support functions will reap economies of scale. This is not wholly supported by the evidence,[17] which suggests that *diseconomies* of scale may set in at a level lower than the size of most district general hospitals. Other arguments for greater concentration frequently rest on unsupported assumptions that greater volumes will lead to better outcomes, or that combining specialist services will lead to improved quality and/or lower average costs (economies of scope). The acute hospital of the future is likely to exist to provide highly specialised care that cannot be provided in the community. Its optimum size will depend partly on the optimum degree of clinical sub-specialisation, which in turn should be informed by more research on volume/outcome relationships and the existence or otherwise of economies of scope.[18]

Diffuse technologies

Health technologies vary in what may be called 'diffuseness'. At one extreme, a drug administered in the form of a tablet or capsule is not very diffuse in this sense; there may be different strengths of tablet, but basically the patient either takes the drug or does not. Even here, there is a degree of diffuseness. Effects may well, for instance, be modified by the level of information provided to him or her and there is evidence that patients entered into clinical trials, irrespective of whether in treatment or control groups, experience better outcomes than those not in trials.[19] At the other extreme of this spectrum, a multi-disciplinary package of care for an elderly person may be very diffuse, with much depending on the precise mix of (say) physiotherapy, occupational therapy, medical and nursing interventions employed, the skill and enthusiasm of these clinicians, and the general morale, resource level and organisational culture of the particular workplace. Somewhere in between these extremes are hernia surgery (where the surgeon's skill is a crucial variable) and paediatric heart surgery (where the anaesthetist's skill and the quality of post-operative care are important). As became evident in the preceding section, such technologies may border on SDO and are also characteristic of such political priority areas as HAZs and HImPs, in which complex partnerships between NHS and other agencies are required in order to deliver multifaceted interventions to populations. Generally speaking, the more diffuse a technology, the greater the problems presented for the conventional forms of HTA using RCTs as described in the first section of this chapter.

These problems can be illustrated by taking a technology which is diffuse, but by no means as diffuse as population-based interventions such as HAZs and HImPs: the 'stroke unit', a term used to denote a system of organised inpatient care which aims to reduce mortality and long-term institutionalisation after stroke. The concept is therefore not one that is well defined, but perhaps the key element is that it is distinguished from what is assumed to be the more usual form of care for such patients, that is on a general medical ward. The diffuseness of such a technology presents a number of obvious problems for evaluation by means of the kind of randomised studies described in the preceding section. First, given the broad definition of the intervention, it is hard for evaluators to be confident that they are aggregating like with like, whether in the context of a primary study or of systematic review or meta-analysis. Thus, stroke units in different hospitals may differ from each other in respect of their policies about how long after the stroke event the patient may be admitted, how long the patient may remain in the unit, the discreteness of physical location, the composition of the clinical team, and the actual micro-level clinical interventions employed. Second, if studies were to show that stroke units reduce mortality and/or dependency (as seems to be the case[20, 21]), the policy consequences would be uncertain; how would one 'roll out' such a technology? Third, since the technology is to some extent social (that is, it implies attempts to modify the behaviour of both staff and patients) it is likely that explanations of its outcome will need to take into account matters of organisational and wider culture, details of which are unlikely to have been collected in research studies. Researchers working within the RCT tradition have sought to address the first and (to some extent) the second of these issues by retrospectively interviewing trialists about the characteristics of the stroke units studied in their original primary research, showing that there is a good deal of homogeneity in their characteristics and that many of these are much less likely to be found in other settings for stroke care.[21]

An alternative research approach to technologies where social change (on the part of staff, patients or carers, or any combination) is central is provided by 'scientific realism', a long-standing philosophy recently popularised in criminological research.[22] The axiom of this approach, which is perhaps closer to a laboratory model of research than is the RCT approach, is that 'causal outcomes result from mechanisms acting in context'. More specifically in the context of *social* change, causation can only be understood:

- as part of the social relations and organisational structures in which it is embedded

- as a product of interaction between agency (the reasoning and choices that individuals make) and structure (their capacity to put these into action)

- as occurring only in the context of favourable social rules, norms, and values

- as occurring within an already self-transforming, rather than static, social system.

Research is thus focused on identifying causal *mechanisms* and the *contexts* in which they operate so as regularly to produce particular *outcomes*. The methodological consequences of this approach are that carefully designed case studies, potentially employing both qualitative and quantitative data, perhaps with controls or comparisons (as 'natural experiments') are likely to be preferred as the vehicle for the development of usable theory, which is in turn the basis of generalisation.[23]

Concluding remarks

RCTs have become a standard method for assessing evidence of the efficacy of health technologies. Such studies have increasingly been combined with various forms of economic appraisal in order to permit more rounded judgements about what healthcare is worth providing, and to whom. The recognition that many health technologies are 'diffuse', alongside concern with SDO questions and the increasing policy prominence of population-based health-related interventions, presents problems for the RCT approach and is likely to lead to a growth of interest in case study and related research methods.

References

1 Sackett DL, Straus S, Richardson WS, Rosenberg W and Haynes RB (2000) *Evidence-Based Medicine: how to practice and teach EBM* (2e). Churchill Livingstone, Edinburgh.
2 Yoshioka A (1998) Use of randomisation in the Medical Research Council's clinical trial of streptomycin in pulmonary tuberculosis in the 1940s. *BMJ.* **317**:1220–3.
3 Treasure T and MacRae KD (1998) Minimisation: the platinum standard for trials? Randomisation doesn't guarantee similarity of groups; minimisation does [editorial]. *BMJ.* **317**:362–3.

4 Schwartz D and Lellouch J (1967) Explanatory and pragmatic attitudes in therapeutical trials. *J Chronic Dis.* **20**:637–48.

5 Fahey T, Griffiths S and Peters TJ (1995) Evidence based purchasing: understanding results of clinical trials and systematic reviews. *BMJ.* **311**:1056–9, discussion 1059–60.

6 Laupacis A, Sackett DL and Roberts RS (1988) An assessment of clinically useful measures of the consequences of treatment. *NEJM.* **318**:1728–33.

7 Egger M, Smith GD and Phillips AN (1997) Meta-analysis: principles and procedures. *BMJ.* **315**:1533–7.

8 Naylor CD (1997) Meta-analysis and the meta-epidemiology of clinical research [editorial]. *BMJ.* **315**:617–9.

9 McKee M and Clarke A (1995) Guidelines, enthusiasms, uncertainty, and the limits of purchasing. *BMJ.* **310**:101–4.

10 Drummond MF (1997) *Methods for the Economic Evaluation of Health Care.* Oxford University Press, Oxford.

11 Williams A (1995) Economics of coronary artery bypass grafting. *BMJ.* **291**:326–9.

12 Mehrez A and Gafni A (1989) Quality-adjusted life years, utility theory and healthy years equivalents. *Medical Decision Making.* **9**:142–9.

13 Department of Health (1999) *Our Healthier Nation.* The Stationery Office, London.

14 Department of Health (1995) *Policy Appraisal and Health.* Department of Health, London.

15 HM Treasury (1991) *Economic Appraisal in Central Government: a technical guide for government departments.* HMSO, London.

16 Goddard M and Ferguson BA (1997) *Mergers in the NHS: made in heaven or marriages of convenience?* Occasional Paper No 1, Health Economics Series. Nuffield Trust, London.

17 Aletras V, Jones A and Sheldon TA (1997) Economies of scale and scope. In: BA Ferguson, TA Sheldon and J Posnett (eds) *Concentration and Choice in Healthcare.* Financial Times Healthcare, London, 23–36.

18 Ferguson BA, Sheldon TA and Posnett J (1997) *Concentration and Choice in Healthcare*. Financial Times Healthcare, London.

19 Stiller C (1992) Survival of patients in clinical trials and at specialist centres. In: CJ Williams (ed) *Introducing New Treatments for Cancer: practical, ethical and legal problems*. Wiley, Chichester, 119–36.

20 Langhorne P, Williams BO, Gilchrist W and Howie K (1993) Do stroke units save lives? *Lancet*. **342**:395–8.

21 Stroke Unit Trialists' Collaboration (1997) Collaborative systematic review of the randomised trials of organised inpatient (stroke unit) care after stroke. *BMJ*. **314**:1151–9.

22 Pawson RD and Tilley N (1997) *Realistic Evaluation*. Sage, London.

23 Yin RK (1994) *Case Study Research: design and methods* (2e). Sage, Thousand Oaks, CA.

10

The NHS R&D Health Technology Assessment Programme

JOHN GABBAY, LYNN KERRIDGE,
RUAIRIDH MILNE AND KEN STEIN

Introduction: the origins of the Health Technology Assessment Programme

Throughout the world, the spiralling demand on limited resources, a better-informed public less willing to trust clinicians' decisions, and the political imperative to deliver a top quality health service have all reinforced the need for evidence-based clinical and policy decision making. At the same time the costs of health technologies have been threatening to over-whelm health services. Yet reliable evidence about existing as well as new technologies has been scarce. The phrase 'Health Technology Assessment' (HTA; *see* Box 10.1) describes one major response to this need. The Office of Technology Assessment in the USA was instrumental in developing the concept of HTA in the 1970s and 1980s, which was more widely adopted in other European countries than in the UK until the establish-ment of an R&D strategy for the NHS in the early 1990s. Yet HTA encapsulates several strands of activity in which the UK research community has been prominent for many years, notably health services research, clinical epidemiology and health economics.[1]

Box 10.1: Definitions

The definition of *health technologies* is intentionally broad and includes all methods used by health professionals to promote health, prevent and treat disease and improve rehabilitation and care.

Health technology assessment is the evaluation of the costs, effectiveness and broader impact of health technologies. As applied by the HTA Programme, it requires the technology concerned to be well defined and beyond the initial stages of development (i.e. HTA is *not* about establishing efficacy, but rather concerned with effectiveness). The end-points of evaluation should be patient-centred outcomes and estimates of the cost effectiveness of alternative technologies. Audit, or surveys of current practice do not normally fall under the remit of HTA.

As recorded in Chapter 1, the publication in 1988 of *Priorities in Medical Research* by the House of Lords Select Committee on Science and Technology[2] acted as a catalyst for the development of the R&D strategy. The government's response to the Select Committee's criticisms was to establish the post of NHS Director of Research and Development to head a new Research and Development Division from January 1991. Later that year *Research for Health*, was published.[3] This outlined the scope of the R&D strategy and emphasised the importance of evaluating the quality, effectiveness and cost of prevention and treatment, and called for more research into the delivery and content of healthcare. Thus, HTA began as one of ten national programmes that, together with the research commissioned by regional health authorities (which in 1996 became the regional offices of the NHS Executive), made up the centrally funded component of the R&D strategy. The structure set up at that time has been described in the previous edition of this book. Since then, however, the context has changed markedly, both in the R&D structure and its NHS environment. The work of running the HTA Programme has been carried out since 1996 by the National Co-ordinating Centre for HTA (NCCHTA), based at the University of Southampton, who are responsible to the Programme Director, originally Sir Miles Irving. The changes in the NHS context have led the new HTA Programme Director, Professor Kent Woods, to alter substantially the way the programme operates. The changing context for other aspects of NHS R&D is dealt with elsewhere in this book. In this chapter we will describe the ways in which the HTA programme, managed by NCCHTA, is now meeting the requirements of its changing context.

The central NHS R&D programme has been restructured so that the original time-limited programmes that dealt with individual care areas such as cancer, maternal and child health, the primary–secondary care interface, and implementing the findings of research have been replaced by three programmes. Although only a small proportion of overall NHS R&D expenditure, HTA is much the largest of the three central programmes, and has a budget in 2000–1 of £7.6m. Its two more recent partners set up in 1998–9 are the Service Delivery and Organisation Programme (SDO; £1m in its first year) and the New and Emerging Applications of Technology programme (NEAT; £300k). These three programmes between them cover all clinical areas and care groups. Yet, like the whole R&D programme, they must now ensure that as far as possible they meet the priorities of the NHS as determined by government, whilst still remaining – as the HTA Programme has always done – responsive to the needs for research as perceived by the NHS itself. HTA, SDO and NEAT, together with the Department of Health's ongoing Policy Research Programme are supported by a Methodology Programme (formerly a subsection of the HTA Programme) and other central resources such as Consumers in NHS Research[4] and the National Horizon Scanning Centre.[5]

The context around R&D has also changed substantially. The new Labour government in 1997 brought about a marked shift to what has become known as the new 'quality agenda', introducing among other things clinical governance, National Service Frameworks, and the National Institute for Clinical Excellence (NICE; *see* Chapter 4). These have all placed increasing demands on HTA to deliver appropriate evidence, but NICE – because it requires assessment of many of the technologies upon which it gives guidance or guidelines to the NHS – has perhaps had the greatest interaction with the HTA Programme (*see* Figure 10.1). It has done so partly because the HTA Programme is particularly well placed to advise on the topics where guidance is most needed, and partly because NICE can lend considerable weight to the implementation of recommendations that emerge from health technology assessments (*see* below). But part of the impact on HTA has also been because NICE needs a faster turnaround of the evidence than the full systematic reviews that HTA has been used to providing. To prioritise, commission, execute, peer review and

Figure 10.1 The HTA Programme.

publish an exhaustively systematic review of the evidence about a technology could take up to 3 years, when decision makers such as NICE may need an answer in less than 6 months. Thus NICE has necessitated a new HTA product, the Rapid Review.

Rapid reviews: Development and Evaluation Committees hand on to NICE

Until 1999 HTA in England was not only carried out at the national level, as described below, but also in NHS regions, three of which had a rapidly responsive method for providing health authorities with reliable information on the cost-effectiveness of health technologies. Known as Development and Evaluation Committees (DECs),[6, 7] they had refined a set of methods of agreeing on important topics requiring urgent policy decisions in health authorities and trusts, providing authoritative reviews within 3–6 months, and so giving health commissioners clear recommendations based on the cost–utility of the technologies in question. The scientific reports for the assessments were systematic but not exhaustive ('quick and clean'), and produced by local academic departments at the Universities of Southampton, Birmingham and Sheffield. They proved remarkably robust considering the speed at which they were produced. For instance, out of a total of 108 reports produced for the Wessex/South and West DEC, none has been found subsequently to be importantly misleading in its conclusions. The DEC teams achieved this by means of clear protocols, which included checking a range of bibliographic databases that always include Cochrane, Medline and Embase; having (latterly) two people to extract data from included studies; and consulting with experts at all stages of the report writing, including peer review of the draft final report. The advent of NICE superseded the function of the

DECs, since NICE effectively performs a similar function for the NHS as a whole. The NICE Appraisal Committee has taken over, at a national level, the role of the former DEC committees. The same academic teams, joined now by the Centre for Reviews and Dissemination at the University of York, continue to produce the scientific reports for the national scheme, which inevitably requires more rigorously executed reports than the regional DECs.

The national HTA Programme commissions this work, whose results, besides forming part of the basis of the guidance from NICE to the NHS on the use of health technologies, are published as fully peer-reviewed academic publications as part of the HTA monograph series. These Rapid Reviews will now form up to half of that series of around 70 issues per year. The other half of the work consists – in roughly equal proportions – of primary research (mainly trials) care and full systematic reviews of the literature, whose prioritisation, commissioning, review and publication form the main work of the HTA Programme. The monograph series also includes all the methodological work commissioned by the HTA and more recently the Methodology Programmes.

The work of the HTA Programme

The purpose of the HTA Programme is to ensure that high quality research information on the costs, effectiveness and broader impact of health technologies is produced in the most effective way for those who use, manage and provide care in the NHS. This requires the programme to be responsive to their needs and to maintain high scientific standards. The HTA Programme has therefore always involved users and providers of healthcare and a wide range of experts to help identify the right questions and to ensure high scientific quality. Thus, the programme differs from most research management programmes in two major respects. First, it is needs-led. Second, it takes a broad view of research management, which involves far more than the commissioning of research. As its logo demonstrates, there are four major components to the HTA Programme (*see* Box 10.2):

- carefully identifying and evaluating gaps in the evidence

- focusing and prioritising research questions

- commissioning research and taking meticulous steps to guarantee that this research answers the original question

- facilitating high-quality peer-reviewed publications which are available to the decision makers at the point of need.

Box 10.2: Processing HTA – the programme's recent activities 1996–99

Identification: NCCHTA received 5950 suggestions for possible HTAs and took nearly 2000 of them forward to expert panels for their help in prioritisation.

Prioritisation: To assist the panels the programme's scientific secretariat wrote approximately 360 briefing papers ('vignettes') and commissioned 72 expert papers. The panels (around 120 people at any one time) submitted 256 priority topics to the Standing Group on Health Technology who selected 171 topics for commissioning.

Commissioning and monitoring: The programme handled 1947 outline proposals and 585 full proposals. This resulted in a total of 258 commissioned projects.

Editing and publication: At the time of writing 204 projects are under way and 72 have been published. To achieve this large throughput of work the programme had to involve around 250 experts in the panels and boards and gave around 2000 items to peer reviewers in the commissioning and publication stage.

Identifying potential topics

The right questions are those that matter to the programme's customers, and which address areas of genuine uncertainty ('evidence gaps'). Although new technologies often meet these criteria, HTA is also concerned with filling evidence gaps in the use of existing technologies, some of which have been routinely used for many years (e.g. depot neuroleptic preparations or preoperative testing). In fact suggestions for evaluation for new and existing technologies tend to be roughly equal in number.

In the past, NCCHTA undertook an annual trawl for topics by sending a mailshot to around 3000 senior staff in, for example the NHS, clinical colleges, scientific societies, research departments, charities and patient groups. In recent years their suggestions have been supplemented by suggestions from other sources. These include research gaps identified in systematic reviews from the Cochrane Collaboration, from the *Database of Abstracts of Reviews of Effectiveness*[8,9] and from NHS R&D projects, including of course the HTA Programme's own research publications (*see* Figure 10.2) This fact, plus the changing roles of other relevant agencies such as the National Horizon Scanning Centre, the National Screening Committee, and the Safety and Efficacy Register of New Interventions and Procedures (SERNIP), have meant that the annual trawl will now be replaced by a single 'widespread consultation'. This is designed to meet the needs not only of HTA but the other central programmes including SDO, NEAT, the Policy Research Programme and NICE. The consultation will be a web-based open channel for suggestions, which will ultimately be accessed through the National Electronic Library for Health. The open channel consultation may be supplemented by targeted consultations with appropriate organisations to achieve more interactive methods of information gathering, including

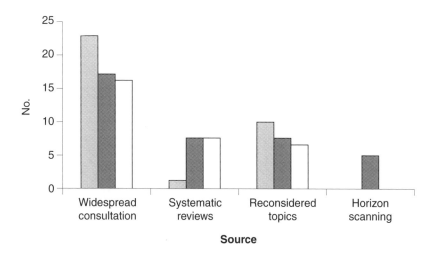

Figure 10.2 Sources of topics prioritised by SGHT.

conference fringe meetings, focus groups, questionnaires and Delphi studies.

Given the necessary lead times involved in commissioning and carrying out HTA – which can take several years – early warning of such technologies is important to ensure that when pressure to use them increases, the right information is available to inform the NHS community on their value. So, whilst the widespread consultation is a good source of topics that are already having an impact or seem imminent, it is also necessary to look further ahead.[10] The National Horizon Scanning Centre (NHSC) is an important and distinct element of the identification process now based at the University of Birmingham.[5] Through a combination of literature scanning (journals and conferences) and consultation with a wide range of individuals and organisations, the NHSC aims to identify technologies which could have a major impact on NHS spending or health outcomes.

Prioritisation and clarification: deciding which topics should be researched

The HTA programme relies heavily on its expert panels (*see* Box 10.2), who help clarify suggestions and contribute directly to decision making at the prioritisation stage. There are now three: the Pharmaceutical Panel, the Therapeutic Procedures Panel, and the Diagnostic Technologies and Screening Panel. Each is a mix of NHS personnel, researchers and health service consumers, who meet three times a year to advise on the priorities for health technology assessment. At each meeting, they receive a list of suggestions that the scientific secretariat have distilled from those received through the identification process and choose a short list for further consideration. The secretariat prepares a briefing paper (or 'vignette') on each of these subjects; for a small number of the more complex topics an expert briefing paper is specially commissioned. Over 1100 clinical, methodological and consumer experts are involved in the HTA Programme as an advisory network for the 'vignettes' and panels, to try and ensure that the decisions about research priorities are based on up-to-date and relevant information.

Consumers of healthcare have been an important part of this process, and NCCHTA now involves them at all stages. Beginning with a pilot to involve consumers in the original expert panels, NCCHTA found that the initial obstacles to full involvement could be overcome with care and effort.[11] All the expert panels now have two consumer members, and consumers give valuable and expert help in preparing vignettes, peer reviewing projects for the commissioning board, and in peer reviewing final reports. This helps to ensure that the HTA questions – and the research results that emerge – are relevant not just to the service providers, but to patients.

The prioritisation process is information-hungry, and with each year of the programme, vignettes have become more structured and comprehensive in response to the demands of the panels (*see* Box 10.3). They allow a more informed discussion at the following meeting where the final priorities can then be agreed for commissioning. In contrast to the old annual cycle,[12] the new panels are able to respond more rapidly to emerging priorities. To date they have recommended in roughly equal proportions primary research studies (involving the collection of new data) and secondary research studies (usually systematic reviews of existing primary studies). The programme can also recommend secondary research in the form of Rapid Reviews (*see* above) to be delivered in a much shorter time than a full systematic review (typically, 3–6 months rather than 1–2 years). Thus, the expert panels are now designed to be more rapidly responsive to emerging problems, the better to meet the needs of the new environment.

Box 10.3: The structure of an HTA vignette

Vignettes usually take the scientific secretariat about 3 days to prepare and involve discussions with up to five experts and searching relevant databases of literature according to a defined protocol.

- **Research question**
  Main question for investigation, plus subsidiaries if required
  Type of research needed

- **Why is research required?**
  Rationale for importance/urgency

- **Who are the patients?**
  Burden of disease
  Type and numbers of patients who may benefit

- **What is the technology?**
  Description, ensuring that it is understandable to non-experts
  Added value of this technology

- **Current and projected use**
  Diffusion rate of this technology
  Comparison with next best alternative

Box 10.3: continued

- **Cost**
  Unit cost of technology
  NHS savings if technology widely diffused

- **Quantity and quality of research so far**
  Appraisal of the evidence
  Includes published research and research in progress

- **What is the potential effectiveness of the technology?**
  Impact of the technology, benefits and harms
  Best/worse case scenarios

- **Additional information**
  Material of relevance to panel decisions, e.g. SERNIP category.

Commissioning: funding work effectively

The aim of commissioning is to turn, wherever possible, the prioritised questions into well-defined projects carried out by the researchers most likely to answer them. To date, commissioning has taken place mainly in two cycles with approximately 40 topics advertised in December and around a dozen in late spring. Under the new arrangements there will be up to 15 topics advertised three times per year. On average, 10 outline proposals are received for each topic and, following assessment by the Commissioning Board members, up to three full proposals are invited. Rapid Reviews work is additional and not subject to the – inevitably slow – commissioning process. It can take up to a year to commission a project once the topic has been agreed as a priority. First, the HTA programme must prepare clear, high quality commissioning briefs and advice to researchers. Then the research community needs time to prepare its outline bids. The HTA Programme must then assess all the many bids that arrive and shortlist them at a Commissioning Board meeting. The selected teams then need to work up their bids to a very high scientific standard, and to ensure that they have put together a multidisciplinary team that will deal with all angles of what are often very complex questions. NCCHTA must then have the applications peer reviewed by appropriate experts (who, because they are often thin on the ground, must be carefully approached so as not to overburden them). The intense scrutiny of the final bids by peer reviewers and the Commissioning Board leads more often than not to modifications to the research protocol – a further necessary delay – which must be finally approved. By streamlining the commissioning process, the programme now commissions virtually all projects within a year of their prioritisation. Although this may seem like a long delay for such high-priority areas, it is vital that the quality of proposals is confirmed through careful consideration and peer review. There are plans to cut the time even further by omitting the stage of outline applications more often, but the disadvantage is the extra work involved for unsuccessful applicants.

All of this is conducted under strict principles of:

- high quality – in advice to applicants, selection of referees, Commissioning Board members and in commissioned work

- openness – so that all decisions are transparent and justified

- equity – treating all applicants with fairness and impartiality

- efficiency – using available resources as efficiently and effectively as possible.

Since the establishment of the NCCHTA, the intensity of commissioning has been increased. By August 2000, 822 research projects had been commissioned. Despite the hiatus in 1999–2000 in the funding of the programme, which caused some of the commissioned projects to be delayed or even superseded, the Commissioning Board now meets three times each year to commission new work. This cycle fits in with the advertisements that follow the three sets of panel meetings. The research projects commissioned cover two kinds of research: primary (involving the collection of new data) and secondary (based systematically on existing research findings).

To date, over 420 proposals for secondary research and 640 for primary research have been received since 1994, which emphasises the size of the task for the Commissioning Board and NCCHTA. Commissioning also relies on the enthusiasm and hard work of a large group of peer reviewers, without whom the HTA Programme would certainly fail to meet its aim of providing high-quality research. Such experts are vital to the success of the programme, but there are clear strains throughout NHS R&D where all programmes are finding it harder to identify potential referees. The HTA Programme is particularly vulnerable to such strain. Because it deals with health care interventions across all specialties and sectors, it must draw on a huge pool of potential referees; and because it is a national rather than a regional programme, it has had to deal with experts who had no prior loyalty to it. NCCHTA has therefore paid particular attention to developing and maintaining the loyalty of its peer reviewers, who are also vital to a later stage of the process, the quality assurance of the final reports.

Monitoring: keeping track of progress

One of the many challenges is to ensure that the question being answered by researchers matches that originally posed by the NHS and honed by the NCCHTA and expert panels. To help with this, the same NCCHTA researchers who prepare vignettes write the commissioning briefs, the chair of the relevant panel checks them, and representatives from each panel sit on the Commissioning Board. Despite this, concerns about 'question drift' are important, especially once the research is under way, when the NCCHTA moves into its monitoring phase. The purpose of this stage is to ensure that work is completed as speedily and efficiently as possible, and that the research meets its intended brief. NCCHTA does this by trying to establish a friendly rapport from the outset. Researchers are required to define the major milestones in their projects and to submit 6-monthly reports to the NCCHTA on a user-friendly form to chart progress against these.

It has been a particular feature of the HTA Programme to arrange site visits to review projects. This happens in projects where the 6-monthly reports suggest the need for review. Visits are also carried out in 'at risk' projects, which experience suggests include those where specific concerns were expressed at the commissioning stage, where several centres are participating in the project, and where the research lasts for more than 5 years. Normally up to 16 projects can be visited this way each year. Every care is taken to minimise the 'inspectorial' nature of these visits. NCCHTA has managed to establish a positive and constructive relationship with the research teams who have often gratefully acknowledged the help and improvement that these visits have brought to their projects. We believe this innovation promotes early identification and resolution of problems.

So far, almost all projects have experienced delays, despite a system of timely reminders from NCCHTA and the Programme Director. This has been partly due to unrealistic timescales being suggested by researchers, particularly in secondary research, which has, over the duration of the programme so far, developed into a much more rigorous and better understood science. The commonest problem encountered in primary research is achieving adequate recruitment rates, and researchers whose proposals reflect greater efforts in planning this element (e.g. through carrying out simple pilot studies of particular approaches) will be at an advantage.

Details of all the work in progress are available in the Annual Report of the HTA Programme and, with more frequent updates, on our website (http://www.ncchta.org). A quarterly electronic bulletin is also available from hta@soton.ac.uk.

Communication: giving people access to good information

Without effective communication, health technology assessment will fail to influence practice or contribute to a knowledge-based health service. It is therefore essential that all projects result in accurate, well-presented peer-reviewed final reports, executive summaries and other outputs accessible by all interested parties. We are not convinced, however, that the NHS would value, or respond to, active dissemination of all the research products of the programme. Only a few topics will be of sufficiently broad relevance and high importance that a proactive approach, including the use of general media, would be appropriate. The Programme's strategy therefore has several strands: the publication of a highly respected monograph series, easily accessible on paper and on the Web both in full and as executive summaries; an insistence on other peer-reviewed articles in appropriate journals, and actively alerting journal editors to the main findings.

When the HTA Programme reaches a 'steady state' about 70 reports will be published each year, and are available in hard copy from NCCHTA or can be downloaded from the web. Box 10.4 indicates the breadth of subject matter represented in those which have been, or are nearing publication at the time of writing in 2000. The publication of a high quality peer-reviewed and well-produced monograph series is essential to the HTA Programme. It is a prerequisite for acceptance onto key databases such as Medline, without

Box 10.4: Some recent and forthcoming topics

HTA monographs. Volume 4 published September 2000

1 The estimation of marginal time preference in a UK-wide sample (TEMPUS) project

2 Geriatric rehabilitation following fractures in older people: a systematic review

3 Screening for sickle cell disease and thalassaemia: a systematic review with supplementary research

4 Community provision of hearing aids and related audiology services

5 False-negative results in screening programmes: systematic review of impact and implications

6 Cost and benefits of community postnatal support workers: a randomised controlled trial

7 Implantable contraceptives versus other forms of reversible contraceptives: two systematic reviews to assess relative effectiveness, acceptability, tolerability and cost effectiveness

8 An introduction to statistical methods for health technology assessment

9 Disease-modifying drugs for multiple sclerosis: a rapid and systematic review

10 Publication and related biases

11 Cost and outcome implications of the organisation of vascular services

12 Monitoring blood glucose control in diabetes mellitus: a systematic review

13 The effectiveness of domiciliary health visiting: a systematic review of international studies and a selective review of the British literature

Box 10.4: continued

14 The determinants of screening uptake and interventions for increasing uptake: a systematic review

15 The effectiveness and cost effectiveness of the prophylactic removal of wisdom teeth

18 Liquid-based cytology in cervical screening: a rapid and systematic review

20 Routine referral for radiography of patients presenting with low back pain: is patient's outcome influenced by GPs' referral for plain radiography?

HTA monographs being prepared for publication

16 Ultrasound screening in pregnancy: a systematic review of the clinical effectiveness, cost effectiveness and women's views

17 A systematic review of the effectiveness and cost effectiveness of taxanes used in the treatment of advanced breast and ovarian cancer

19 RCT of non-directive counselling, cognitive-behaviour therapy and usual general practitioner care in the management of depression and mixed anxiety and depression in primary care

21 A systematic review of wound management: Antimicrobial agents for chronic wounds; Diabetic foot ulceration

22 Using routine data to complement and enhance the results of randomised controlled trials

23 Coronary artery stents in the treatment of coronary artery disease.

which the visibility of the Programme's outputs would be severely curtailed. It provides easy access to NHS staff and other users. Finally, it ensures that universities and HEFCE accept the outputs of HTA, because they are highly cited publications on Medline and Embase, as high-quality research for inclusion in the research assessment exercise. Otherwise, research teams would be disinclined to undertake HTA projects, or indeed to help so willingly in providing expertise in prioritisation, commissioning and peer reviewing.

Publication in peer-reviewed journals is now also a contractual requirement of researchers funded by the HTA Programme. This will bring research to the attention of clinicians in particular, and will provide a technical summary of the specific aspects of the project, accessible by searching major reference databases. Modern publishing practice accepts that such dissemination, provided it is done openly and with the intention of delivering appropriate messages to different target audiences, does not constitute duplicate publication. On the contrary, it allows the busy clinician or policy maker to read about the relevant findings, while also ensuring that the full peer-reviewed findings are available for more in-depth information, and fully open to scientific scrutiny.

Third, as part of the editorial process for HTA, executive summaries of the reports are prepared and widely disseminated to targeted audiences. These provide a concise and coherent description of the work, highlighting key findings, and are particularly suitable for a non-technical readership. They are placed on our website (http://www.ncchta.org). From these, the 'bottom line' on the evidence for health technologies can readily be identified.

Challenges for the future

From a standing start in 1993, the UK has now established the largest publicly funded portfolio of HTA research in the world. As the products of commissioned projects become more numerous, the value of the Programme should be felt at all levels of the NHS and throughout the international health care community. But significant challenges remain.

First, it is vital that the work of the HTA Programme becomes more widely known about and used throughout the NHS. This requires that the Programme's products continue to be seen as timely, relevant and useful by the key stakeholders, who include health service users as well as policy makers, managers and clinicians. The balance between central and 'bottom-up' priorities must therefore be maintained.

Second, much remains to be done to ensure that the HTA findings are optimally communicated, in a range of appropriate formats, to all the relevant stakeholders. However, the key to developing a knowledge-based health service is not in creating or summarising the knowledge but in developing a culture that values information and facilitates its use. The proliferation of journals, courses and workshops promoting 'evidence-based practice' from a bottom-up perspective and the emphasis placed on clinical governance by the Department of Health and imaginative responses in some areas suggest that such a culture is developing.

Third, all steps must be taken to ensure that the research community continues to regard the Programme as prestigious and worthy of their serious involvement. This in turn means that the quality of the research and the programme's outputs must be kept as high as possible, and that the requirement for timeliness as against thoroughness does not compromise the reliability and hence the reputation of HTA.

Fourth, HTA must develop its links even more closely with other initiatives to improve the quality of healthcare. Producing high-quality HTA evidence and disseminating the results are only a very small part of implementing change. The greatest remaining challenge is to make better use of the knowledge to improve care.[13] However, the 'quality agenda' is establishing better organisational structures, which will make it easier to manage the use of knowledge in the NHS. Much of the output from the HTA Programme has great relevance to the National Service Frameworks for care,[14] to the work of the 'Czars' responsible for major areas such as cancer and mental health, to the new processes of clinical governance, continuing professional development and re-accreditation, and to the commissioners of healthcare. It is crucial to persuade these and other agencies to build research evidence from the HTA Programme into their thinking. After all, the HTA Programme has been designed to help remove uncertainties, and to fill the evidence gaps felt most keenly by those delivering healthcare interventions across the whole range of NHS services. As the evidence about cost effect-iveness emerges, the new NHS structures should surely make more use of it. NICE has shown the lead in this respect, and has done much to take the outputs of the HTA Programme and turn them into guidance and guidelines likely to affect practice and policy in the NHS. However, this is only one of the mechanisms by which the evidence can be brought to bear in NHS policy, and much still remains to be done to make the best use of the emerging evidence from the HTA Programme.

References

1 Stevens A and Milne R (1997) The effectiveness revolu-tion and public health. In: G Scally (ed) *Progress in Public Health*. The Royal Society of Medicine Press, London.
2 House of Lords Select Committee on Science and Tech-nology (1988) *Priorities in Medical Research*. HMSO, London.
3 Peckham M (1993) *Research for Health*. Department of Health, London.
4 www.hfht.org/ConsumersinNHSResearch.
5 http://www.hsrc.org.uk/horizon/.
6 Stevens A, Colin-Jones D and Gabbay J (1995) Quick and clean: authoritative health technology assessment for local health care contracting. *Health Trends*. 27(2):37–42
7 Best L, Stevens A and Colin-Jones D (1997) Rapid and responsive health technology assessment: the development

and evaluation process in the South and West region of England. *J Clin Effect*. **2**:51–6.

8 http://agatha.york.ac.uk/darehp.htm.

9 http://www.cochrane.de/.

10 Robert G, Stevens A and Gabbay J (1999) 'Early warning systems' for identifying new healthcare technologies. *Health Technol Assess*. **3**(13):99 (monograph).

11 Oliver S, Milne R, Bradburn J *et al*. (2001) Involving consumers in a needs-led research programme: a pilot project. *Health Expectations* (in press).

12 Stein K and Milne R (1998) The NHS Health Technology Assessment Programme. In: M Baker and S Kirk (eds) *Research and Development for the NHS: evidence, evaluation and effectiveness* (2e). Radcliffe Medical Press, Oxford, 67–85.

13 Getting Evidence into Practice (1999) *Effective Health Care Bulletin*. **5**(1). NHSCRD, University of York.

14 http://www.doh.gov.uk/nsf/nsfhome.htm.

11

Service delivery and organisation research: a new national programme

MAUREEN DALZIEL

Introduction

The Service Delivery and Organisation R&D Programme is a new national programme of research and development that is funded by the NHS. Its purpose is:

To produce and promote the use of research evidence on how the organisation and delivery of services can be improved and to contribute to improved population health.

The aims of the programme are to:

- ensure that good research-based evidence about the effectiveness, cost effectiveness and equity of different models of service is available and accessible

- generate the evidence base to encourage managers and others to implement appropriate change

- identify and develop appropriate R&D methods

- promote the development of expert R&D capacity and

- involve service users and other stakeholders in the R&D programme.

Areas of work

The programme's four main areas of work are to:

- identify and prioritise themes and topics for R&D

- commission R&D to fill key gaps

- collect, evaluate and synthesise evidence from relevant R&D around the world

- make R&D evidence available, and work with others to promote access and uptake.

History

The NHS R&D Programme was initiated in 1991 to improve the research base for the NHS. Currently, around £65m is spent on this programme. In addition, there is R&D support for NHS providers (£384m) and the Department of Health commissions research through its own, separately funded (£30m) Policy Research Programme to inform ministerial policy and priorities.

The allocation and management of NHS R&D funding is about to change after widespread consultation. The NHS R&D Programme and the national R&D programmes within it will form a key part of the new NHS Priorities and Needs R&D funding system.

There are currently three main national R&D programmes:

- Service Delivery and Organisation (SDO)

- Health Technology Assessment (HTA)

- New and Emerging Applications of Technology (NEAT).

These three major programmes are underpinned by two groups: the Consumers in NHS Research Group, a sub-group of the Central Research and Development Committee (CRDC), which advises on the best ways to involve consumers in NHS research; and the NHS Methodology Programme, which incorporates the activities of the HTA Programme's former methodology panel and expands this to support all aspects of NHS R&D.

NHS policy context

The NHS is undergoing a programme of reform at present and a Health Bill has gone through Parliament (the 1999 Health Act). The White Papers *The New NHS: modern, dependable*,[1] *A First Class Service*[2] and *Saving Lives: our healthier nation*[3] have outlined the Government's strategy for health improvement and healthcare delivery around the theme of modernisation. After further consultation a national plan for the NHS has been published. Principles and initiatives that have emerged to date include:

- broader perspective of health than just health services

- working in partnership to improve and deliver healthcare across organisational boundaries is encouraged

- Health Action Zones and new structural arrangements for primary care and initiatives for re-organising services to provide the best quality of care for patients, their carers and relatives have been introduced

- a number of National Service Frameworks for particular groups of patients (e.g. mental health and coronary heart disease)

- clinical governance, a process designed to improve accountability for the quality of services delivered has been introduced

- some new direct patient access services e.g. NHS Direct have been introduced.

Over the years there have been requests from NHS managers and health professionals that more of the R&D levy should be spent to support:

- research to enable processes of care to be designed to deliver modern effective care to the users of the service

- research evidence that informs policy and management decisions

- research knowledge that can be made use of by those who use and deliver healthcare

- NHS organisations such as the Commission for Health Improvement (CHI) and the National Institute for Clinical Excellence (NICE) to address some of the important issues that they have or will have to grapple with, if they are to meet expectations.

What is SDO research?

The term *health service delivery and organisation* in relation to research is very broad. It could therefore include service delivery and organisation issues for any condition or user group. It potentially includes all healthcare sectors – preventive, primary, secondary and tertiary.

Areas of SDO research might include:

- service delivery issues and models of care, e.g. comparing different models of mental health services; user involvement

- organisational issues at different levels, e.g. at the level of teams (such as primary care); or departments; or whole organisations; and the interfaces between organisations

- appropriate settings for care, e.g. primary or secondary

- management of change and implementation issues in health-care organisations.

The SDO research would not usually include questions concerning:

- individual treatments or interventions

- population health interventions

- interventions that help reduce health inequalities.

A review carried out by the Office for Public Management[4] suggests that almost 20% of the health service research funded by the NHS is SDO.

The National Co-ordinating Centre for NHS Delivery and Organisation Research and Development (NCCSDO)

In April 1999, the London School of Hygiene and Tropical Medicine was awarded the National Health Service Executive (NHSE) contract to support the National SDO R&D Programme and to ensure its aims are achieved. It supports the Director by providing a coherent national focus for SDO R&D. Its main tasks include identifying and prioritising topics, commissioning research and project management and linking and networking with a wide range of stakeholders including those that make use of, deliver and determine health services, as well as those who manage and conduct research.

National listening exercise

During Autumn 1999, the NCCSDO carried out a national listening exercise which brought together a wide range of stakeholders in focus groups around the country and in some expert groups, using structured discussions within a common framework.

The purpose of this exercise was to enable the SDO R&D Programme to understand what issues are most important to those delivering and organising services, and to those receiving them and to secure their ownership of the Programme.

A wide range of people have been consulted during this process including service users, healthcare professionals, health service managers, researchers and others.

The findings were debated during January and February 2000 with a wide range of policy makers and experts in the field. A total of 354 people have been consulted in person during this process (*see* Appendix for breakdown of participants). A recent listening exercise conducted by NCCSDO, as detailed in the report *National Listening Exercise – Report of the Findings*,[5] identified the following themes for the SDO R&D Programme:

- organising health services around the needs of the patient

- user involvement

- continuity of care

- co-ordination/integration across organisations

- inter-professional working

- workforce issues

- relationship between organisational form, function and outcomes

- implications of the communication revolution

- the use of resources, such as ways of disinvesting in services and managing demand

- implementation of major national policy initiatives such as the national service frameworks for coronary heart disease and mental health.

There was agreement that priority should be given to reviewing existing research knowledge within and outside of the health sector on the themes rather than just to commission primary research. There were requests for tools that could be applied at the local level. These may require some joint projects or working with others who have an organisational or personal development responsibility or an education and training brief.

Commissioning and managing SDO R&D

The important components for the effective commissioning and managing of SDO R&D include:

- guidelines, systems and accountability to ensure that work of high quality and value for money is delivered rapidly

- a commissioning process that encourages innovation and development, together with the best of current SDO methodologies to provide clear answers to researchable questions

- a process that identifies and exploits opportunities arising from planned developments in the service

- a link between the research community and front line staff and users to ensure relevance and promote uptake of research findings.

A 30-person Commissioning Board for the SDO R&D Programme (made up of service users, healthcare professionals and health service managers with representation from associated research funding bodies, research programmes, researchers, and the NHS Executive) is being set up under the chairmanship of a practising senior NHS manager supported by an academic vice-chair. A first meeting of the Board took place in the Summer of 2000. The Board will, amongst other things:

• engage with users, healthcare professionals and researchers

• oversee the development of the national SDO R&D Programme

• assess and approve research applications

• steer the communication of the results of this research across the health service, to other individuals and organisations with influence and leverage on healthcare delivery, including service users

• develop a case for resources in this area of research

• act as a conduit to influential networks and connections across the NHS, research institutions and universities.

As this area of research is so different from the traditional biomedical research there are a number of new commissioning mechanisms that may be valuable for addressing the challenges of SDO R&D.

• *Partnership development model.*[6] (*see* Figure 11.1). In this model the funding body acts as a facilitator and brings together researchers, policy makers and healthcare practitioners to agree a process which is research robust but able to yield results that can be applied either as policy or in healthcare delivery. It has been tested in North Thames on a range of SDO issues such as human immunodeficiency virus/acquired immune deficiency syndrome services, the clinical workforce and screening. The advantages of this method are that there can be fast generation of a useful result and it encourages partnerships between users, health care professionals and researchers.

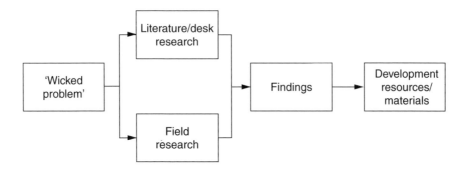

Figure 11.1 The partnership development process.

- *Iterative model.* This method involves appointing a Director of Research with a support committee that oversees the whole evolution of a research area or process. It is possible that it may be engaging of healthcare professionals but costs more to support the process and there are risks that it will not be considered open nor be research robust.

Ideal outcomes from any R&D commissioning process would build SDO R&D capacity if possible, ensure that research findings are taken into widespread practice and are able to be applied in many different healthcare organisational contexts easily.

Change management and quality improvement

In the Policy Paper on quality improvement, *A First Class Service*, the NHS SDO National R&D Programme was charged with providing a review of existing research findings 'of relevance to change management and quality improvement in the NHS'.

Given the agenda on action for quality set out in *A First Class Service*, the aim of this review is to provide organisations within the NHS with evidence of what works and what does not in terms of change management.

The objectives of these projects are:

- to map out the main theories of change management which have been set out within both the private and public sectors, and provide a user-friendly summary of these

- to provide a comprehensive review of empirical evidence of change management in healthcare at the macro, meso and micro levels

- to outline the gaps in our knowledge and what further work might be usefully carried out in this area.

Continuity of care

Continuity of care was one of the themes that emerged from the national listening exercise.

A scoping exercise is underway, the aims of which are to:

- advise the SDO R&D Programme on what further R&D should be commissioned in this area

- map existing research on continuity of care from the patient's perspective

- include any evidence found concerning the organisational implications of implementing continuity of care

- include evidence from healthcare fields and from any relevant related fields, e.g. social care.

The development of methods of SDO R&D

Research on the service delivery and organisational aspects of healthcare is a vital component of the improvement of health services. However, while research on health service delivery and organisation has been carried out over recent years funded through the NHS R&D Programme and others, the major focus of the health services research programme, has been health technology assessment (HTA). Associated with this has been the development of methods to evaluate health technologies and the development of a 'hierarchy of evidence' as proposed by the Cochrane Collaboration for systematic reviews. These developments have tended to prioritise quantitative methods, and in particular randomised controlled trials. The establishment of the national SDO R&D Programme has signalled that there is a need to develop methods and tools to enable researchers to address SDO R&D.

There is a view that a broader range of methods needs to be considered for providing evidence on SDO issues.

The NCCSDO with the NHS R&D Methodology Programme is preparing a book for publication in the autumn of 2001 on methods for SDO. This research will be used to develop guidelines to inform the commissioning process and to guide research applicants of SDO R&D.

Communication

NCCSDO will develop a communication strategy that reflects the findings of the listening exercise (*see* above):

- briefings will be targeted at health service users, managers, professionals, policy makers and those with an education and training background in addition to the research community, using a range of processes

- information on all final reports and outputs will be entered into appropriate databases and library systems including the NHS Electronic Library for Health and Learning Networks

- the SDO R&D Programme website will be developed further to enable prompt and interactive feedback from health service users, managers and professionals

- the communication strategy will build on the NHS Executive's Central R&D Committee's current and future thinking on dissemination in liaison with the regional offices of the NHS Executive and other commissioned programmes.

References

1 Department of Health (1997) *The New NHS: modern, dependable*. HMSO, London.
2 Department of Health (1998) *A First Class Service*. HMSO, London.
3 Department of Health (1999) *Saving Lives: our healthier nation*. HMSO, London.
4 Barker J (2000) *A Review of Existing NHS Service Delivery and Organisation Research and Development Projects*. Office for Public Management, London.
5 Fulop N and Allen P (2000) *National Listening Exercise: report of the findings*. NCCSDO, London.
6 NHS Executive (North Thames) (1998) *Health Leading the Agenda: developing and sustaining partnerships in reality*. NHS Executive (North Thames), London.

Appendix I

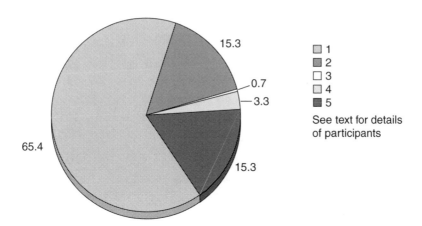

Figure AI1.1 Listening exercise participants as a percentage.

Key to categories of participants in Figure AI1.1

1 Public/users
   Consumer representatives
   Hospital clinical staff
   Primary and community clinical staff
   Middle managers
2 Senior managers
   Public health specialists
   Policy makers*
   Local authority (social services)
   Innovators
3 Non-executive directors
4 Educators
5 Researchers
   Research and development
   Research funders

Analysis of attendance at SDO focus groups

Rank	Abbreviation	Category	Number	%
1	P	Public/users	11	4.0
1	CR	Consumer representatives	42	15.3
1	H	Hospital clinical staff	54	19.6
1	C	Primary and community clinical staff	21	7.6
1	MM	Middle managers	52	18.9
2	SM	Senior managers	20	7.3
2	PH	Public health specialists	7	2.5
2	PM	Policy makers*	*	
2	LA	Local authority (social services)	3	1.1
2	IN	Innovators	12	4.4
3	NED	Non-executive directors	2	0.7
4	ED	Educators	9	3.3
5	RES	Researchers	20	7.3
5	RD	Research and development	13	4.7
5	RF	Research funders	9	3.3
	Total		275	100.0

The ranking is as recommended by the Expert Forum. The numbers and percentages relate to the actual participants in the focus groups held.

*The findings of the focus groups were debated by the Expert Forum and at two dinners held for policy makers and people with an interest in the NHS at national level, including representatives of the media, voluntary sector, local authorities and non-executive directors of NHS organisations. Together with the First Expert Forum, this included 79 people, giving a total of 354 people consulted during the Listening Exercise.

Key to categories

C	includes GPs, health visitors, district nurses	NED	non-executive directors of health authorities and trusts
CR	includes CHCs, consumer organisations, voluntary organisations, carer representatives	P	includes patients and carers
		PH	includes both medically and non-medically qualified public health specialists
ED	representatives of education consortia, medical education, nurse education, pharmaceutical education	RES	researchers based in academic institutions
		RD	includes regional directors of R&D, other R&D staff and research nurses
H	includes front line hospital medical and nursing staff, ambulance staff, paramedics	SM	includes trust and health authority chief executives, executive directors and acting directors (including directors of public health)
IN	includes successful change implementers in the NHS		
MM	includes ward managers and sisters, business, operations and service managers		

12
New and emerging applications and technologies

MARK R BAKER

Introduction

The NHS R&D New and Emerging Applications of Technology (NEAT) programme was established in 1998 as one of the three core national programmes alongside Health Technology Assessment and Service Delivery and Organisation. It was always envisaged that NEAT would be smaller than its sister programmes and that it occupied a niche position between commercial research and development and the implementation of relevant technologies within the NHS setting.

The main aim of NEAT is to use applied research to promote and support the use of new or emerging technologies in order to develop healthcare products and interventions. Priorities for the selection of technologies and for funding research focus on those potential applications that will enhance the quality, efficiency and effectiveness of both healthcare and social care. The NEAT Programme will commission and support both strategic and applied research with the basic principles of NHS R&D funding being adhered to. Of particular importance in this programme is the ability of applicants to demonstrate that the technologies concerned are capable of being applied to a defined health or social care need and that the outputs of the research must be generalisable across those settings.

NEAT in context

The NEAT Programme was developed in order to overcome a specific development barrier. In doing so it also fills a perceived funding gap among other R&D funding streams. While much of the R&D programme is concerned with the delivery of evidence-based medicine and the development of knowledge to support the implementation of NHS priorities, the NEAT Programme is specifically involved in bridging the gap between the development by industry of products and processes that could then be put back into the health service and their implementation into the NHS for proven benefit. The NEAT is informed by the horizon scanning centre which was established following the NHS White Paper *The New NHS: modern, dependable* in 1997. Under the recent proposals for funding R&D for NHS priorities and needs, NEAT forms part of the innovation theme for generating knowledge for health, alongside clinical research and R&D to support technology transfer.

When the national field R&D programmes (mental health, cancer, heart disease and stroke, etc.) were being restructured in 1997, it was recognised that a gap existed in the range of activities which were to be supported by the Health Technology Assessment and Service Delivery and Organisation Programmes. This gap was particularly marked at the interfaces between the government Research Councils and the NHS and between the NHS and the various industries whose products are used in healthcare. NEAT does not offer a safety net for failed Research Council applications nor does it provide a substitute for funding of product development for which the industries themselves should take responsibility.

Nor does it fund work involving fully developed products and interventions which are already in use in the NHS. Many of the successful applications for the NEAT Programme so far involve the novel application of technology for health purposes.

Management of funding

Unlike the other national R&D programmes, NEAT is managed directly from the Department of Health. The programme manager (Dr Peter Greenaway) is advised by a programme advisory committee that is composed of experts, policy makers and representatives of the consumers. The Advisory Committee advised that the uniqueness of the NEAT Programme and the lack of experience of managing and commissioning research in this field suggested that the first call for proposals should be held on a responsive basis only. This would enable the programme managers to obtain an estimate of the demand for the programme and so that areas of major interest from the perspective of potential researchers could be identified and assessed. Formal commissioning arrangements within the programme are so far at a much more limited level than in the other national programmes.

The original budget identified for the NEAT Programme was £1 million per annum for 5 years. The first call for proposals generated an over-subscription of 60-fold of the funds available. A large proportion of the proposals, understandably, fell outside the very narrow niche that the managers of the Programme had identified for NEAT funding but the exercise demonstrated how heavy the demand for funding research is in this area.

The Programme so far

The NEAT Programme is open to all research providers in the academic and NHS communities who may apply on an individual basis or as part of an active collaboration. Joint funding arrangements with other research funders, exceptionally including commercial interests, may also be acceptable. The initial call for proposals in February 1999 generated almost 300 outline proposals for funding, of which only five were initially approved (*see* Box 12.1). It is anticipated that further proposals from these original applications will also be supported and that other modes of commissioning will be developed as experience in the field rises and as the horizon scanning centre begins to generate specific fields of interest.

Box 12.1 NEAT Programme: projects approved in 1999

- An automated multiplex detection system for prenatal screening of haemoglobinopathy mutations.

- Screening for left ventricular systolic dysfunction using novel cardiac-derived peptides.

- High-intensity focused ultrasound therapy for localised prostate cancer: assessment using real-time magnetic resonance imaging and *in vitro* spectroscopy.

- Treatment of unilateral spatial neglect using contingency electrical stimulation.

- Speech recognition for people with severe dysarthria.

All R&D budgets have been squeezed in recent times, partly to protect mainstream spending on health service delivery and partly to ensure that adequate funds are made available to the Service Delivery and Organisation Programme, while the overall NHS R&D funding system is being revised and restructured. The NEAT Programme is likely to remain a substantially lower priority than the other core programmes (Health Technology Assessment and Service Delivery and Organisation) and other innovative developments by the present government including the development of cancer research networks and further investment in public health R&D.

Future prospects for the NEAT Programme

Although the NEAT Programme was developed to fulfil a genuine and specific niche within the spectrum of R&D funding it requires a particularly strategic approach to R&D to justify its retention within the NHS R&D programme. The relatively low priority which it can expect to enjoy during the current administration's lifetime suggests that alternative approaches will be adopted to bridge the gap between technology development and its identification by horizon scanning and the conversion of the technologies into useable products for healthcare. Indeed it is even questionable whether this work needs to be conducted in the NHS or indeed in the UK at all. Two possible approaches to the future of the Programme come to mind. First, if a body of technologies emerge which require funding in this transitional area to translate into useful products in the NHS, and the bridging R&D funding is not readily available, the commercial interests themselves may sufficiently lobby the government of the day to resurrect the Programme and enhance its status. Alternatively, a formal collaboration between the government and various health-related technological industries may provide a less formal and also less controlled approach to bridging the gap between technology development and technology applications.

The NHS and its staff have a long history of involvement in technology development much of it by doctors and scientists working in hospitals. However, most of this work has been informal and is undoubtedly underrated by the NHS hierarchy as a whole. Formal funding of the type of research that leads to the development of prototypes has never been likely to be widely supported within the NHS, given the other pressures on funding. Hence the need to identify specific priorities and niches for funding this type of work, and to do so preferably in partnership with the generating industries and the leading edge-service providers.

The future of such programmes is dependent far more on political interest, and perhaps commercial lobbying, than on the needs or benefits of investing in such research. Unfortunately, benign political environments occur by chance and not necessarily when they are most needed.

Note: Members of NEAT were invited to write this chapter but declined.

13
Methodological research

RICHARD LILFORD AND DAVID BRAUNHOLTZ

Introduction

The risk of stroke is reduced by de-furring carotid arteries;[1] pre-school educational interventions improve the long-term prospects for economically deprived children;[2] 'business process re-engineering' is as likely to impair as to improve service delivery.[3] Each of the above statements is backed up by evidence. In each case, the evidence seems to call for action; surgeons should unblock arteries, government should provide pre-school education in deprived communities and managers should resist the recent fad for business process re-engineering. However, in none of the above cases, does the evidence have the status of absolute truth; in each case, questions could be asked about reliability (are the inferences true for the context in which they were obtained) and validity (will they be true in another [similar but not identical] context). Judgements about reliability and validity turn on the method used to obtain and analyse data. Thus, moving from information (data) to decisions requires appreciation of methodology. Methodology thus underpins the whole concept of 'evidence-based practice'. As the recent intense controversy over screening for breast cancer has shown[4] design of clinical studies is crucially important. The truth of the matter, however, is that the theoretically optimum design is frequently limited by logistic or ethical considerations. The logic of this is that a study design which would be considered severely sub-optimal in one setting, may be the best that can be achieved in another. Results may therefore be subject to unavoidable potential bias even in studies of high quality in the sense that they are as good as possible. A judgement has to be made about whether or not such potential bias invalidates the study completely. If not, and since no study can be perfect, further judgement is necessary about the extent of the putative bias; remembering always, that bias might apply in the context in which the study results were obtained (diminishing reliability) or between the context in which they were obtained and that where they might be applied (diminishing validity). It follows from this, then, that methodology is crucially important not only in the design of studies, but in their interpretation. If this argument is accepted, then two corollaries pertain:

1 the quality of health policy and medical decision making depends as much on how scientific results are interpreted as on how they are produced, and

2 the users of scientific results, cannot abrogate their responsibility to understand the characteristics of different research methods (i.e. the methodology); whether or not we believe that certain kinds of genetically modified food are harmful to health or that the BSE crisis is abating, *depends* on appreciation of the methods by which results were obtained.

The notion, therefore, that the application of scientific results can be divorced from methodology is simply naïve – implementing evidence-based practice is as much a function of appreciation as application. An understanding of these principles, explains why the NHS R&D Programme has, from its inception, incorporated a strand of methodological research.

What is methodological research?

Methodological research is research into research; it is the ancient form of inquiry, with roots in philosophy, which tries to understand, not what is true, but how we may know the truth. The huge advances in Western science in the last 400 years are entirely contingent upon advances in the underlying Methodology; looking back from the 21st century, it seems curious that for centuries the advance of science was held back – indeed, held in check – by failure to appreciate that understanding nature required empirical observations of nature. But observations are often not enough – comparisons must be made. Control groups were mentioned in the Book of Daniel, but the idea laid dormant until the 14th century and really only came into widespread use in the 19th century. Although, in that century, there are one or two references to the idea of selecting people for treatment 'by lot', randomisation came into medical practice in the middle of the 20th century. Statistical methods have developed to enable probabilistic inferences to be made from observational studies. In the 18th century the Reverend Thomas Bayes worked out how to qualify the improvement in our knowledge about the truth, resulting from an observation. This method has been used for the interpretation of diagnostic tests ever since. However, in the last 10 years there has been a surge of interest in the use of Bayesian probability theory to interpret comparative studies in general and clinical trials in particular.[5] The Methodology Programme within the NHS R&D Programme has sought to keep British clinical research at the cutting edge intellectually, by making sure that it is underpinned by epistemological inquiry. Indeed, this becomes an ever-greater need, as policy is increasingly made at national level, so that any errors are likely to be magnified.

Types of methodological research

Producing a typology is always difficult, because there are many different ways of splitting a subject, each with advantages and disadvantages. However, it seems reasonable to begin by saying that there are two kinds of methodological (epistemological) inquiry: the first is philosophical analysis – thought experiments; the second, empirical investigations.

Let us deal first with philosophical inquiry. This can be broken down into two broad categories: mathematical/statistical inquiry and pure philosophical reasoning. Examples of the former include the review of methods for analysis of cluster trials.[6] A larger number of studies involve philosophical analysis. An example is studies of the ethics of clinical trials, involving exegesis of the 'uncertainty principle' as the ethical basis for clinical trials – a term which can be shown to be rather slippery, since it implies merely absence of certainty.[7] It is noted, however, that much methodological research is a mixture of philosophical and statistical analyses. An example, is a study of Bayesian methods in clinical research,[8] which deals with both the epistemological basis of Bayesian thought and with practical advice on how to operationalise Bayesian statistics. Similarly, the authoritative analysis of methods for systematic reviews[9] contains a mixture of epistemological and statistical argument.

Turning to empirical investigation, we would recognise two broad 'types'. First, and most easily distinguished, are studies based on the collection of primary data. Leaving aside the use of case studies to illustrate philosophical concepts, such studies may be based on qualitative or quantitative data. Qualitative studies would include, for example, studies in which patients were asked how they felt about taking part in clinical trials (reviewed Edwards et al. (1998)).[7] Primary quantitative studies are usually designed to answer second-order questions in methodology – questions about how to use a method rather than which study design to use. Thus, there are trials of different methods of entering patients into clinical trials,[7] studies of different methods to increase response rates to questionnaires[10] and studies to compare quality of life on different scales.[11]

Empirical studies bearing on the reliability and validity of different types of study design are usually based on secondary research. Secondary research involves information collected from published output. This may simply consist of a review of other methodological studies – whether of a philosophical or empirical nature. We call this the use of literature as data. However, the literature is increasingly used as a source of data to compare results by study design – that is, studies conducted for one purpose (to test effectiveness) are used for another purpose (to compare the results of effectiveness research by methodological type). In order to do this, articles are grouped by topic, and then, by method used. Results by method, are then compared across topic. One of the classic studies of this type compared the results of historically controlled studies with those using contemporaneous controls,[12] showing that there is a systematic tendency for the historically controlled studies to produce much greater estimates of treatment effect size. The rise of meta-analysis has greatly facilitated this sort of enquiry and classic examples include the studies of Schultz and colleagues[13] and Moher and colleagues,[14] which compared the results of randomised trials by various quality criteria, such as the rigour of the randomisation process, blinding of outcome and completeness of follow-up. More recently still, a large number of studies have compared the results obtained from large, clinically rich databases and randomised trials, showing that these do not deviate as wildly as some people had previously thought.[15,16] Such studies will be of immense importance as greater opportunities arise to exploit the patient's electronic record. There is, of course, a philosophical issue underlying such comparative studies; when comparing the results of one methodology with another, a view needs to be taken about which results are the most reliable. However, since the whole purpose of the venture is to determine relative reliability of methodologies, interpretation of results is problematic. In order to break the regress, it is necessary to make one or two assumptions. For example, it can be assumed that the methodology that produces the most conservative results is the most reliable or a 'gold standard' can be chosen. For example, in the above study by Schultz and colleagues,[17] secure randomisation produced results which were, on average, 30% more conservative than those produced when random-isation was less rigorous.

Making use of the results of methodological research

The Methodology Programme of the NHS R&D function has placed a lot of emphasis on making sure that the results of methodology research are taken up in practice. For example, each project report, if accepted, is published as a monograph. Second, the *British Medical Journal* has published a book[18] summarising the main contributions. Lastly, Sage has pub-lished an extensive handbook of methodological research, based on programme output.[19] Thus, the first method that is used to ensure that methodological projects have high impact is to make sure that they are well disseminated through the publication route, and also that they are available electronic-ally – indeed, the Methodology Programme reports receive a high number of hits on their website.

In addition, the output from the programme is scrutinised by the Methodology Group, for any specific policy implications, which go beyond general enlightenment and consciousness raising. For example, the finding[17] that the quality of random-isation is crucial to research reliability has led to the firm policy recommendation that all clinical trials funded by the

R&D Programme, should use a system of third party random-isation, unless there are compelling counter arguments – for example, research in remote corners of tropical countries. The discovery that giving people more information at the time that they are offered entry into clinical trials results in higher anxiety and lower acceptance rates, combined with the further evidence that the more somebody knows about trials before they are offered entry into a particular trial, the less likely they are to be alarmed, has produced the strong advice that understanding clinical trials should be incorporated in current programmes attempting to improve the public appreciation of science.[7]

Some of the recommendations emanating from Meth-odology Reports evoke sufficient societal consensus for immediate policy making – the importance of third party randomisation, being an example. Other output will result in gradual enlightenment and incremental changes in practice rather than wholesale changes in policy – a good example is the growing use of Bayesian methods. Yet other output may be highly controversial and may even seem 'wacky' by the standards of today. An example here, is the analysis purport-ing to show that data monitoring committees should no longer meet *in camera*, but that interim data should be made widely available.[20] The Methodology Programme will not give official support to such radical ideas, but also makes no attempt to suppress them, given that the research programme should prepare the NHS for possible future worlds, not just the currently accepted paradigm.

There are some reasons to think that the Methodology Programme is already having an influence on practice, even where it has not been able to write explicit policy statements. One example is the area of fast-changing technologies, where the right moment to start a clinical trial may be hard to define. A Methodology Report suggested that evaluation should start earlier rather than later,[21] and this idea was developed further into the 'Tracker Trial' concept , whereby an evaluative clinical trial would be used, not only to compare generic new methods, but also various sub-types.[22] Already, this methodology has been largely incorporated in a major Health Technology Assessment study of endovascular aneurysm repair (EVAR). The Methodology Programme has commissioned work on modelling in the design of clinical trials, and in determining their value for money. However, the first author has already used this methodology, to determine value for money of a proposed £20 million trial of screening for ovarian cancer. The funding of this trial was secured on this basis, as well as the intrinsic scientific merit of the proposed study.

One of the main challenges of methodology research, is the evaluation of service delivery and policy at the community level; for example, evaluation of micro-economic interventions (single regeneration budgets, 'New Deals' for communities, etc.). There are few examples of cluster experiments, and one of the challenges for the UK is to follow the US lead of developing policy around an evaluation strategy, including randomisation of intervention and control sites. In the absence of this, it is necessary to 'fall back on' naturalistic designs, and compare outcomes across intervention and non-intervention sites, and intervention sites of different types and/or exposed to different forms of the intervention. Before and after measurements allow change, rather than absolute levels of attainment, to be compared and this makes causal inferences more secure. However, problems remain. First, statistical power may be low, especially in crucial sub-groups. Second, even when before and after measurements are made, bias cannot be excluded. Finally, views about the success or failure of the intervention may depend on integrating different types of knowledge, including the very plausibility of what is being done and the results of qualitative research design to understand how interventions are perceived. All of these problems can be analysed within the Bayesian paradigm and more work on this is urgently required.

References

1 Cina CS, Plase CM and Haynes RB (2000) Carotid endarterectomy for symptomatic carotid stenosis (Cochrane Review). The Cochrane Library issue 1. Update Software, Oxford.

2 Zoritch B, Robert I and Ley A (2000) Day care for preschool children (Cochrane Review). The Cochrane Library issue 1. Update Software, Oxford.

3 Walston S and Borg R (1999) The effect of re-engineering: fad or competitive factor. *J Health Care Manag.* **44**:456–74.

4 Gotzsche PC and Olsen O (2000) Is screening for breast cancer with mammography justifiable? *Lancet.* **355**:129–34.

5 Lilford RJ, Thornton J and Braunholtz D (1995) Clinical trials and rare diseases – a suggested way out of a conundrum. *BMJ.* **311**:1621–5.

6 Ukoumunne OC, Gulliford NC, Chinn S *et al.* (1999) Methods for evaluating area wide organisation based interventions in health and healthcare: a systematic review. *Health Technol Assess.* **3**(5).

7 Edwards S, Lilford RJ, Thornton J and Hewison J (1998) Informed consent for clinical trials: in search of the best method. *Soc Sci Med.* **47**:1825–40.

8 Lilford RJ and Braunholtz DA (1996) The statistical basis of public policy: a paradigm shift is overdue. *BMJ.* **313**:603–7.

9 Sutton AJ, Abrams KR, Jones DR *et al.* (1998) Systematic review of trials and other studies. *Health Technol Assess.* **2**(19).

10 Edwards P, Clarke M, Diguiseppi C *et al.* (2000) Methods to influence response to postal questionnaires (Cochrane Review). The Cochrane Library. Update Software, Oxford.

11 Fitzpatrick R, Dowey C, Buxton MJ and Jones DR (1998) Evaluating patient-based outcome measures for use in clinical trials. A review. *Health Technol Assess.* **2**(15).

12 Sacks H, Chalmers T and Smith H (1982) Randomised versus historical controls for clinical trials. *Am J Med.* **72**:233–40.

13 Schultz KF, Chalmers I, Hayes RJ and Altman DG (1995) Empirical evidence of bias. Dimensions of methodological quality associated with estimates of treatment effects in controlled trials. *JAMA.* **273**(5):408–12.

14 Moher D, Pham B, Jones A *et al.* (1998) Does quality of reports of randomised trials affect estimates of intervention efficacy reported in meta-analyses? *Lancet.* **352**:609–13.

15 Britton A, McPherson K, McKee M *et al.* (1998) Choosing between randomised and non-randomised studies: a systematic review. *Health Technol Assess*: **2**(13).

16 Benson K and Hartz AJ (2000) A comparison of observational studies and randomised controlled trials. *NEJM.* **342**(25):1878–86.

17 Schultz KF, Chalmers I, Hayes RJ and Altman DG (1995). Empirical evidence of bias. Dimensions of methodological quality associated with estimates of treatment effects in controlled trials. *JAMA.* **273**(5):408–12.

18 Black N, Brazier J, Fitzpatrick R and Reeves B (eds) (1998) *Health Services Research Methods*. BMJ Books, London.

19 Stevens A, Fitzpatrick R, Abram J *et al.* (2001) *Advanced Handbook of Methods in Evidence Based Healthcare*. Sage, London.

20 Lilford RJ and Braunholtz DA (2000) Who's afraid of Thomas Bayes? *J Epidemiol Comm Health.* **54**:731–9.

21 Mowatt G, Bower DJ, Brebner JA *et al.* (1997) When and how to assess fast changing technologies: a comparative study of medical applications of four genetic technologies. *Health Technol Assess.* **1**(14).

22 Lilford RJ, Braunholtz DA, Greenhalgh R and Edwards SJL (2000) Trials and fast changing technologies: the case for tracker studies. *BMJ.* **320**:43–6.

14
Improving research through consumer involvement

HARRY CAYTON AND BEC HANLEY

In the mid 1990s, researchers and clinicians at Mount Vernon Hospital in Middlesex were concerned about heavy use of the breast cancer outpatients' clinic, which was causing long waiting times. They planned to shift some of the work back to a primary care setting, and designed a research protocol to help address this. Before beginning the study, they asked women who used the clinic for their views on the research. The women said that they had not realised there was a problem with the clinic, and that they did not want their care transferred to their GPs – on the whole they had more confidence in their hospital consultant. The women suggested other solutions to the problem, such as the development of a speedier access system and the increased use of support nurses.[1] In response to these suggestions, a speedier access system was developed. Clinicians and researchers have gone on to involve consumers extensively in R&D at the hospital, for example in the development of guidelines on breaking bad news.[2]

Sometimes it seems that the obvious people to ask about research – those who are usually on the receiving end of it – are ignored. This can often be at great cost to the NHS. By involving consumers, as in the example above, we believe that research can be more relevant to the needs of consumers, more reliable and more likely to be used (*see* Box 14.1).

This chapter outlines some of the reasons for involving consumers in R&D, gives some pointers about how to involve consumers and explains something about the role of Consumers in NHS Research, the group which has been set up to advise on how best to involve consumers in R&D in the NHS. We have also included some examples of collaborations between consumers and researchers.

Box 14.1: Consumers

Consumers are:

• patients

• carers and parents

• long-term users of services

• organisations representing consumers' interests

• people who are the recipients of health promotion campaigns

• people asking for research because they believe they have been exposed to potentially harmful circumstances, products or services.

There is no single term used by these groups to describe themselves, and there are many different definitions of the term 'consumer'.[3]

Why involve consumers in R&D?

There is a great need for systematic evaluation of the impact of consumer involvement in research in order to demonstrate its value. However, there are numerous examples that illustrate how the involvement of consumers can improve both quality and relevance within the research and development process.

The experience of Mount Vernon Hospital, mentioned above, showed the importance of involving consumers in the identification of research topics. Consumers can also play an important role in prioritising topics for research, bringing a more outcome-focused perspective (*see* Box 14.2). Evidence suggests that clinicians are not able to act as proxies for consumers in this area, as clinicians and consumers have different priorities for research. A recent review has shown that such differences are very common and can be quite dramatic in scale, especially when there is little dialogue between clinicians, consumers and researchers.[4] The involvement of consumers in prioritising topics for research by the Health Technology Assessment Programme (*see* Chapter 10) has, according to those involved, improved the research prioritisation process for everyone.[5]

Box 14.2: Alzheimer's Society quality research in dementia

In 1999 the Alzheimer's Society restructured its research grants programme to give people with dementia and carers a powerful role in its structures and procedures.

The Society was concerned to ensure:

- research was relevant to the needs of users and carers

- research funds were used in the most targeted way

- that quality of life was central to research objectives

- that dissemination was aimed at changing and improving practice

- that research and its results were accessible to the public as well as to professionals.

The involvement of people with dementia and carers is requiring the Society to develop new ways of working and communication. Empowerment training is being provided and the Internet is being used to enable participation. Partnership between professional researchers and people with dementia and carers is stimulating new thinking.

Consumers can also improve the design of a research study. Consumers in NHS Research has recently commissioned a survey looking at the involvement of consumers in randomised controlled trials (RCTs) in the UK. Those responsible for co-ordinating trials have reported that consumers have been particularly helpful in the development of the trial protocol, ensuring that it is 'patient friendly' and that the trial will work in practice. Some researchers believe that consumer involvement in RCTs can also help to boost recruitment.[6]

Some consumers undertake research themselves, for example, acting as interviewers in qualitative studies. This can ensure that the views of groups which are often marginalised, such as those from black and minority ethnic communities, can be accessed.[7]

Involving consumers in disseminating the results of a research project can help to ensure that recommendations are implemented. Many voluntary organisations carry summaries of the latest research in their magazines for members, written in accessible language. Voluntary organisations can also work to ensure that people receive care based on the latest research evidence. For example, the UK Breast Cancer Coalition produced a leaflet for consumers, highlighting best practice, much of which had not been consistently implemented across the NHS. This enabled women to identify and ask for an improved standard of care.[8]

As well as practical reasons there are ethical reasons for involving consumers in research. All researchers have a duty to ensure that their work is as good as they can make it and ethically constructed and managed. Consumer involvement requires a shift in attitude from people as passive subjects of research to active participants. This will help to ensure a broader ethical perspective and to enable informed consent to research.

How to involve consumers in R&D

Although experience shows that the involvement of consumers can improve the quality and relevance of research,

Consumers in NHS Research has found that this is not a cost-free or time-saving process. The suggestions outlined in Box 14.3 are drawn from a publication[9] which aims to give some guidelines to researchers on involving consumers in their work. See the 'further information' section at the end of this chapter for more information on how to obtain this.

Box 14.3: Key steps to involve consumers in research and development

- Take time to develop relationships with consumers.

- Develop a 'job description' to outline the role of consumers within the research.

- Make time for consumers to prepare and participate.

- Be prepared to adjust your plans in response to consumer views.

- Budget for the additional cost of involvement.

- Where possible and appropriate, involve consumers from the beginning of the research.

- Keep them informed throughout the project.

- Involve consumers in planning for and undertaking dissemination.

- Ensure you involve consumers in evaluating the research and the involvement of consumers within this.

Perhaps the most important ingredient in successful collaboration between researchers and consumers is the development of good relationships. Researchers need to understand the priorities and ways of working of consumers as well as ensuring that their own priorities and working methods are transparent and clear. Clarity about the aims and objectives of a research project will enable both partners to develop a brief 'job description' to think more clearly about who might be involved.

Many researchers struggle with the question of which consumers they should involve. Sometimes the answer is more obvious than others. For example, if a project involves elderly people a researcher might seek to involve pensioners' associations or Age Concern groups as well as approaching individual elderly people with whom the researcher may already have worked. In other studies, it might be appropriate to contact a local community group, self-help or advocacy group, or Community Health Council.

Some researchers express concerns about the 'representativeness' of consumers who may become involved in a project. This is usually a misplaced concern. Similar questions are rarely asked about how representative a doctor or other professional on a research team is of all doctors or all nurses. It is more helpful for the researchers to think about consumer *perspectives* rather than consumer *representatives*, and to focus on the role that the consumers will have within a project. For example, if a researcher is looking to ensure that the outcome measures of a research project are of relevance to women with breast cancer, it would be appropriate to involve those who have experience of this condition. A local or national breast cancer support group may be helpful in identifying these consumers. And a self-help group or voluntary organisation will also be helpful in offering support and advice to the consumers involved. It is always important to involve more than one consumer, so that individuals do not feel isolated and unable to contribute. It can be very daunting for consumers to challenge the views of experienced professionals, however well intentioned.

Some consumers are becoming increasingly interested in the degree to which they will be involved in the research, and it is important to be clear about this from the outset. There are a number of models to describe degrees of involvement, the best known of which is the ladder of participation developed by Arnstein.[10] In Figure 14.1 we illustrate a simplified model of degrees of involvement, which should be seen as a continuum.

| Consultation | Collaboration | Control |

Figure 14.1 Degrees of consumer involvement.

In this model, *consultation* involves asking consumers for their views, and using these views to inform decision making. *Collaboration* involves at least some degree of shared decision making, whilst user-*controlled* research involves consumers taking responsibility for the research, with 'professionals' acting only in an advisory or technical capacity at their request. The collaboration model is becoming increasingly popular within R&D in the NHS, as it allows both researchers and consumers to make a contribution to the research process. At a conference organised by Consumers in NHS Research in January 2000 there was also growing interest in the potential impact of consumer controlled research.

Different degrees of involvement will be appropriate to different research projects. This will be determined by, amongst other things:

- the nature or discipline of the project
- the intended outcome
- the relationship between researchers and consumers
- the requirements of the funding body.

Because consumers have a valuable contribution to make to the identification and prioritisation of research, they should be involved from this early stage if at all possible. It is also important to budget for consumers to be involved in the research. It can be extremely disempowering to be the only person involved in a research project who is not paid for this. Even if consumers choose not to accept payment, it is important to budget for travel expenses, childcare/carer costs and payment for involvement at a minimum. If you are involving consumers with particular needs, you may also need to consider budgeting for interpreters or translators, hire of accessible venues, etc. If you are asking consumers to undertake part of the research, or consult with others, costs for postage, photocopying and telephone bills may also need to be built in.

It is important to keep consumers involved throughout a research project, and not to wait until the dissemination stage to give results to those likely to be most affected by them – consumers. Results of research should be fed back to those who have taken part. Report positive, negative and inconclusive results, not just those consumers may want to hear. This should be done before the results are published in the media (*see* Box 14.4). Once the research is complete, it is important to involve consumers in a review of the research and their involvement in it. An evaluation of the role of consumers can provide useful information and encouragement for other researchers wishing to involve consumers in their work. It can also help with the more effective involvement of consumers in future projects.

Consumers in NHS Research

Much of the information and guidance offered within this chapter has been developed through, or by a group called Consumers in NHS Research (formerly the Standing Advisory Group on Consumer Involvement in the NHS R&D Programme). This group, which consists of consumers, researchers, research funders and those working within health and social care, was set up in 1996 to advise on how best to involve consumers in R&D in the NHS. It is formally a subcommittee of the Central Research & Development Committee.

Box 14.4: Involving consumers in the dissemination of the results of a RCT

The Concorde trial, the first drug trial for human immunodeficiency virus (HIV) in the UK, began in 1988. It compared azathioprine (AZT) with a placebo and aimed to test whether AZT could postpone or prevent the onset of HIV-related disease. The results showed that there was little difference between using the drug in the early or later stages of the HIV infection.

The results of the trial were controversial and had significant implications for those who had taken part in the trial, as well as for others affected by HIV/acquired immune deficiency syndrome (AIDS). It was therefore important that participants and clinicians caring for people with HIV/AIDS understood the results prior to press releases. The Medical Research Council, which co-ordinated the trial, had already collaborated with consumer groups in the HIV/AIDS field and had built up successful working relationships with them. A regular newsletter was used throughout the trial to keep participants informed about progress and a consumer was also on the panel that was responsible for breaking the results.

The Terrence Higgins Trust was involved in the trial steering group. Their member was involved in meetings with consumer groups. These meetings took place over several months and continued after the release of the results to ensure that those affected by HIV were not misled by inaccurate media reporting.

Consumers in NHS Research aims to ensure that consumer involvement in R&D in the NHS improves the way in which research is prioritised, commissioned, undertaken and disseminated. In order to do this, it is:

- developing strategic alliances with key groups to encourage shared learning and networking to promote consumer involvement in health research

- empowering consumers to become involved, through the provision of information, conferences and training

- monitoring and evaluating the effects of consumer involvement in NHS R&D to ensure that consumers are effectively involved, and that this involvement leads to improved research.

The group has commissioned a number of studies, including a database of health research projects in which consumers have been actively involved and a review of consumer involvement in research in other, related fields such as social care and the environment. It also offers advice and guidance on consumer involvement in health research to all parts of the NHS R&D Programme, researchers and consumers.

Box 14.5 Involving consumers in R&D in a local NHS trust

The South London and Maudsley NHS Trust has involved consumers extensively in the research undertaken within the Trust. Two consumers sit on the local research ethics committee. Consumers who sit on the steering committee of the Centre for Rehabilitation in Severe Psychosis (CRISP) have been instrumental in shifting the emphasis towards outcome measures related to general functions, including social functioning levels and quality of life as opposed to symptom reduction.

Consumers have also been involved as researchers. For example, in an evaluation of medication education groups for acute inpatients at CRISP, a consumer acted as a researcher, attending the groups and acting to assure that the research was of a high quality. A manual is now being developed collaboratively by a consumer, a pharmacist, and a clinical psychologist.

In other areas of the Trust, researchers have worked with self-help groups and support groups as well as voluntary organisations to ensure research is relevant to the needs of consumers. A meeting of local consumer groups has recently been convened to discuss research priorities and to consider how consumers might become further involved in the planning and conduct of research.

The future

Over the last few years there has been increasing involvement of consumers at all stages of the research process, and in small-scale studies as well as large multicentre trials. However, despite growing evidence of the benefits of consumer involvement and policy guidelines encouraging it, some researchers still continue to exclude those who have most to benefit, and often most to contribute to research – the users of health services. One task for the future is to convince these researchers and research commissioners of the benefits of consumer involvement. There is also much to learn about the best ways to involve consumers, the most effective stages at which to involve them and the training required for consumers and researchers to ensure that this type of collaboration is effective.

The phrase 'knowledge is power' may be a cliché but ignorance is undoubtedly powerlessness. There is nothing as powerless as a patient. Anxious, weak, perhaps in pain and often deprived of clothes, usually cowed into submission by lengthy waiting, and almost always ignorant of what is wrong and what will happen, patients are rarely in a position to be active consumers, and to demand evidence-based healthcare. You cannot be an active consumer without the power of information.

Consumer involvement therefore is part of the building of evidence-based medicine – medicine that is relevant to the real needs of patients and their carers. The NHS needs to continue to build knowledge-empowered communities based on collaborations between consumers, researchers and clinicians, to ensure that patients and doctors can make decisions based on real evidence, not on ignorance.

Further information

More information about involving consumers in NHS research can be obtained from the Consumers in NHS Research Support Unit, Help for Health Trust, Highcroft, Romsey Road, Winchester, SO22 5DH. Tel: 01962-872247. E-mail: conres@hfht.org. Website: www.hfht.org/Consumers inNHSResearch.

References

1 Bradburn J, Maher J, Adeweyi-Dalton R *et al.* (1995) Developing clinical trial protocols: the use of patient focus groups. *Psycho-oncology.* **4**:107–12.

2 Walker G, Bradburn J and Maher J (1996) *Breaking Bad News.* King's Fund, London.

3 Blaxter M (1995) *Consumers & Research in the NHS.* NHS Executive, London.

4 Grant-Pearce C, Miles I and Hills P (1998) *Mismatches in Priorities for Health Research between Professionals and Consumers PREST.* University of Manchester, Manchester.

5 Oliver S, Milne R, Bradburn J *et al.* (2001) Needs and feasibility study for developing consumer involvement in the NHS R&D Health Technology Assessment Programme. *Health Expectations.* **4**(1):18–28.

6 Epstein S (1996) *Impure Science.* University of California Press, Berkeley, CA.

7 Johnson M (1998) *The Involvement of Black and Minority Ethnic Consumers in Health Research and Development: A report to accompany the SAGCI databases.* University of Warwick, Warwick.

8 UK Breast Cancer Coalition (1998) *Save this leaflet and it could save your life.* UK Breast Cancer Coalition, London.

9 Hanley B, Bradburn J, Gorin S *et al.* (2000) *Involving Consumers in Research & Development in the NHS: briefing notes for researchers.* Consumers in NHS Research Support Unit.

10 Arnstein S (1969) Ladder of citizen participation *J Am Inst Planners.* **35**:216–23.

15
NHS R&D: future prospects

MARK R BAKER

Introduction

Evolution is the key to long-term survival. As the political, professional, economic and service context changes, so the imperative for flexibility and adaptability in R&D leadership increases. The short-term future seems to be secure but, in the longer term, further adaptation will be required to ensure the continuation of an internally driven, evidence-based NHS. Here we will consider the major drivers for long-term changes of direction and purpose in the NHS R&D strategy.

Political leadership

At the present time, and for the next couple of years at least, political priorities for the NHS focus on improving the operation of the NHS and not on high-level change. The NHS Plan attempts, unsuccessfully, to eliminate the debate on how to pay for healthcare in the UK. However, the debate will re-emerge with every crisis and/or change of political power. For now, however, the focus will be on doing the basics better and much less so on bringing new tricks into patient care.

With political leadership concentrating on downstream NHS performance, it is very unlikely that high-level R&D will interest policy makers. Disenfranchised, demoralised and disillusioned managerial leadership in management does not augur well for the future impact of R&D on either policy or practice. Furthermore, there is growing suspicion that politicians are using knowledge selectively to support or justify political decisions which have already been made. For example, the NHS Plan, which covers a set of spending commitments over 3 years, flags up the prospect of introducing national screening programmes for prostate cancer and ovarian cancer despite the fact that government-sponsored trials will not report until the second half of the decade. Indeed, there is a sense of major discomfort that government policy is anticipating the genuinely uncertain outcome of its own research.

The only bright spot on the horizon is the government's active support for the emerging national R&D programme in Service Delivery and Organisation. Even here, however, it could be interpreted that there is a degree of cynicism about the government's motives in backing the SDO Programme, hoping to use its medium to back their own predetermined initiatives in focusing on micro performance issues in NHS delivery.

Implications of changing the funding arrangements for NHS R&D

The prime motivation behind changing the internal funding mechanism for NHS R&D has been the need to improve value for money and return on investment. During the negotiations over the future arrangements for funding research in the NHS, there was real fear that the whole strategy would be cancelled in order to recycle the 1% of NHS spending which is used for research to strengthen the funding of services. This was never likely to be the outcome, at least in its entirety, although a major part of the funding was at risk. In the event, a decent compromise has been reached and the outcome, hard won as it was, is fair and reasonably positive.

Own-account research

The large majority of NHS R&D funding has always been tied up in the Culyer formula for funding task and portfolio research in NHS Trusts. This recycled the funds formally tied up in the 25% research element of SIFTR and the research subsidy to London's postgraduate teaching hospitals. However, the post-1996 system of allocating funds only marginally improved the utilisation of these resources, most of which was still used for own-account research. The radical redesign of funding systems described in Chapter 5 is a response not only to the need to focus investment in a manner that supports political objectives but also to the exasperation with the low added value of most own-account research. Compared with the structured national and regional commissioned pro-grammes of R&D, own-account research was much less likely to result in publication, or citation or to attract funding for further research. There are exceptions but they are too few to justify the continued spending of so much of the budget on this mode of research. A more structured approach, it is argued, will lead to a higher research output of better quality.

For the ultimate funders of research – the taxpayer via the government – these arguments are irresistible. However, there is a price to pay when any choice of this nature is made. A more centralised approach to research funding, based as it will be on active and proactive commissioning, will inevitably reduce the engagement of local clinicians of all professions in primary research. The development of inclusive R&D networks, such as that being developed for cancer trials, will help to overcome these difficulties but there is no doubt that the barriers to involvement of most clinicians in research have been raised significantly.

In many ways, the current changes towards increasing central direction of research are a natural consequence of a national R&D strategy and constitute little more than an evolution step in the history of the strategy. The consequences for individual researchers of low productivity are a regrettable but inevitable step in the march of progress. It is to be hoped that the changes lead not to disengagement of clinicians from the R&D strategy but to a more collaborative approach to research of real importance for the future improvement of healthcare.

The introduction of clinical governance into all levels of the NHS ought to assist the implementation of research outputs into practice. However, the managerial basis of clinical governance (Chief Executives of NHS organisations are the accountable officers) may perversely lead to a less desirable approach. Clinical governance implementation is beset with bureaucracy and it risks becoming just another set of boxes to tick in the invasive performance management culture. Together with the outputs from the National Institute of Clinical Excellence, National Service Frameworks and other government guidance, clinical governance is in danger of being just a tool of management in promoting those aspects of evidence-based practice which fit with political priorities. The acquisition of knowledge in its own right, as a general good, is no longer regarded as a necessary or even desirable goal.

Managers and managing

The understandable medical dominance of the R&D strategy since its inception has proved a two-edged sword. The current unpopularity of the medical profession with politicians has not served the interests of R&D. In addition, the intellectual snobbery of medicine and of researchers, while not universal, has served to exclude senior management to a large extent from the R&D leadership. What involvement there is tends to be tokenistic and has done little to overcome the innate anti-intellectualism of NHS management.

The underlying problem has its origins in the creation of general management in the NHS in 1984 and the emergence of a line of management accountability which the government could use while bypassing the professions. Not all managers are guilty; those who perceive the need to understand the varying cultures and values of their staff groups find themselves torn between the career-determining simplicity of government targets and the rectitude of a hearts and minds approach with their whole organisation. Continuing central-isation of power and policy, which has been a feature of the last 15 years, will further compromise the relationship between management, professions and researchers. Only a radical rethink and redesign of the NHS will overcome this. These difficulties are not unique to the NHS but are character-istic of national health systems. It is the uniqueness of the NHS R&D strategy which heightens its negative consequences in this country.

The price we pay in the UK for having a comprehensive nationalised healthcare system funded out of general taxation is the expectation by politicians that they can dictate what is done with their investment. This has to be acknowledged as inevitable and wishing it away won't help. Given the similar challenges faced by other healthcare systems, it probably does not matter in the long run. Advocates of a knowledge culture in the NHS, stimulated by involvement in research itself, will have to function within the political environment of the day and remain adaptable to changes in both style and priorities. The goal of reducing the lead time between the emergence of relevant knowledge and its incorporation into practice is shared by all NHS stakeholders. What is clear is that a better informed public will, one way or another, demand success in this goal. Politicians, as well as managers and clinicians must be alert to the culture change in society which their policies are stimulating and supporting.

Index